The BLUELINE *Anthology*

The BLUELINE *Anthology*

Edited by

Rick Henry, Anthony O. Tyler,
Stephanie Coyne-DeGhett, Myra Gann,
Alan Steinberg, *and* Alice Wolf Gilborn

SYRACUSE UNIVERSITY PRESS

Library of Congress Cataloging-in-Publication Data

The blueline anthology / edited by Rick Henry . . . [et al.].— 1st ed.
    p. cm.
  ISBN 0-8156-0770-9 (pbk. : alk. paper)
  1. American literature—New York (State)—Adirondack
Mountains Region. 2. American literature—New York
(State)—Adirondack Mountains. 3. Adirondack Mountains Region
(N.Y.)—Literary collections. 4. Adirondack Mountains
(N.Y.)—Literary collections. 5. New York (State)—Literary
collections. 6. Mountain life—Literary collections. 7. American
literature—20th century. I. Henry, Richard.
  PS548.N7B58 2004
  810.8'097475—dc22   2003027037

At treeline, all complexity
falls away
and you can see clear
to the blue line
of beyond.

    —Pamela Lee Cranston
       from "Coming to Treeline"

CONTENTS

Poetry

Prose

PREFACE

Editing an anthology culled from more than twenty volumes of a literary journal is different from editing the journal itself. Selecting poetry and prose for each issue certainly involves a great deal of sifting, reading, and rereading. But there are great numbers of submissions that can be omitted by default: the authors have little understanding of the journal and its mission and have submitted work that is inappropriate (or of insufficient quality). The pool from which the poetry and prose in this anthology, however, has already passed that test. Indeed, the original proposal to Syracuse University Press was twice the size of the present volume. The authors of many of the works in that proposal, especially from the early years, simply couldn't be found, no matter how wide we cast our net. In the end, what we have is an anthology of works that continued to reward our time spent rereading them. For that, we are grateful to their authors. But we are also grateful to all of the writers who have contributed to *Blueline* over the years. In many ways, this is a tribute to their creativity and continued engagement with those concerns that the journal holds dear.

Also deserving thanks are all of the people who have worked on the journal—all of them volunteers. In addition to the six editors whose names can be found under the title of the anthology, the following have all served editorial roles in one form or another: Jane Z. Carroll, Helen Collins, Tracy Meehan, Michael Nerney, Autumn Blanchard, Christopher Shaw, Paul Corrigan, Gary McLouth, Kate O'Connell, Janet Moulton, Hallie Bond, Michele Pinard, C. Shaw, Warren Jefferis, Marlene Youmans, Jonathan Dallas, Tony S. Cook, John W. Cross, Janice Londraville, Richard Londraville, Warren Wigutow, Robert G. Foster, Jon Chatlos, Homer Mitchell, Maurice Kenny, Dan Mills, Dana Henry, and Anna Gerhard-Arnold. The following have given freely of the their time and expertise in the production of the journal: Rosine Lemon, Jan McL. Day, Eleanor King, Pamela Jones, Dorothy Swanson, Sally Bowers, Betty Helmsworth, Anne Iott, Sallie Bailey, Richard Storms, Toby Schoyer, James L. Swedberg, Stephen Summer, Faye A. Serio, Pete Baker, Patric Cohen, Ruth Sullivan, and Suzanne Lebeda. A number of students have worked as interns for the journal, many of whom contributed directly to the production of this volume: Amy Parker, Kimberly M. Evans, Katina Morse, Brandy Langlois, Joseph McGhee, Pamela Lunz, Carrie Thomas, Leilla Brooks, Jason Emerson, Jamie McKenty, Chris Kenny, Amy Donohue, Cindy McBride, Rebecca Mersand, Michele Reardon, Michelle Yaworski, Alyssa Wood, Amanda Hanley, Cindy Harland, Richard Baldwin, Gabe Boswell, Heather Robson, and Debra Washburn.

Special thanks go to Karen Wilson, who, in addition to serving as managing editor of the journal for the past several years, was the main coordinator of the project through the original proposal. We are also grateful to the State University of New York at Potsdam for their past and future support, and, of course, the people at Syracuse University Press, who are ever helpful.

INTRODUCTION

Blue Suite—Six Editors on the Line

A Gift over Time

I look at the poetry in this anthology as a portfolio of work that gives, richly, the gift that all portfolios can: the gift of time. Time is one of the subtle dimensions of any literature, for only over time does it become fully itself and deepen, developing both history and direction. Much of poetry is apprehended in discrete chunks of time: it is composed in its own moments of clarity and connection; it is submitted to journals and contests; it finds a life on the printed page. Volumes of *Blueline* have quietly accumulated for over two decades, the poetry of each year sitting in its separate volume, bound to its year both in its pages and in how we choose to read it. What if? is the question a portfolio asks. What if we, instead, hold these works together? It is the same question an art museum asks when it pulls together twenty Winslow Homer watercolors never before exhibited in the same place. What if an art gallery invites a dozen paintings by Don Wynn from private collections for a show? What will we see that we didn't see before, even though we might have been familiar with each individual work before? I once walked into a room in Canada's National Gallery in Ottawa that was filled with the landscape paintings of their Group of Seven. How powerful to view them that way, together. They became, metaphorically, a landscape of their own. I have discovered, as selections were made to represent *Blueline*'s poetry, that these individual works, too, combine to create a poetry landscape of their own.

I have seen each individual poem in this *Blueline* anthology before. Each chosen poem is read more than once, discussed among editors, read again. I read each issue when it comes out. Sometimes I pull out a poem to share with my creative writing classes. (Elizabeth Biller-Chapman's haiku sequence comes to mind, as does Robert Hunter's "Fish's Car.") Sometimes when a new poem is accepted from a poet we have published often—like Matthew Spireng or Eric Ormsby or M. J. Iuppa—I'll go back and reread, for enjoyment, pieces of theirs that have found their way into print with us in previous years. None of this, however, is the same as seeing all these poems stand together, *Blueline*'s voices over time.

These poems take on a resonance from each other—and take on an added dimension over time as this poetry accumulates. Between these covers, pieces written over twenty years occupy the same moment by becoming part of the same book. Implicit in this gift of time that an anthology gives is the gift of making it new. When we see these poems and consider them side by side, what does it make us see that we might not have otherwise thought about before? What new ideas emerge from this new poetic landscape? Here, then, I think, is what we at *Blueline* have been quietly up to, one reading season after another: we have been creating a place for this poetry to develop its collected resonance. How many poems does a region need before it has a sense of having a poetry of its own? *Blueline,* over the years and in this volume in particular, has practiced the quiet art of binding together a literature that is of this place, by spirit or by geographic claim. Each of these poems, individually compelling, becomes more revealing as a work among works—as one of the pieces that accumulate toward a contemporary history of regional writing. Why not, asks an anthology, why not bring this poetry all together, if only for the astonishing pleasure of seeing it whole?

Stephanie Coyne-DeGhett

Nephew of the Circus

When I was a boy in Worcester, I couldn't wait for the circus to come to town every year. My uncle was the road manager, so we always got tickets in the front row. We also were entertained in his plush railroad car, his traveling home. I witnessed his various activities as manager firsthand. I didn't grow up to be a circus manager, but editing *Blueline* for nearly a decade has not been unlike. First the performers had to be selected. The presentation of their acts had to be arranged. The ring had to be provided. Customers had to be solicited. The show must be staged and, finally, evaluated.

In selecting the performers for *Blueline,* we conducted a national talent search. I had the help of my ringmasters and their assistants in this process.

Myra Gann was in charge of selecting the exciting prose performers for the main ring and Stephanie Coyne-DeGhett directed the choosing of the high-flying aerialists, the poets. We were wise enough to retain the outstanding performers inherited from the founder and previous manager, Alice Gilborn. These artists who continued to perform during my tenure formed an outstanding core. However, we were always seeking and finding new talents which gave the show the piquancy of the new. Fluctuations in the availability of various types of performers kept our work stimulating.

Once the acts were engaged, getting them before the public provided different kinds of challenges. I always enjoyed arranging the order of presentation, shut up in my office for hours. Myra Gann created the design for the acts, the layout. The late Pete Baker assisted in transmitting the design and the layout to the word processor. Year in and year out, mounting the production provided the most surprises, from discovering that acts that we thought to be original had already been performed elsewhere, to checking before show time only to find the backdrops, the illustrations, had been placed upside-down.

Looking back, friendships established with the performers and with those who assisted me in preparing the show stand out the most after of a decade behind the cover. I did not expect now to see the best of the performers, in our judgment, come back for an all-star show. Such an encore is satisfying beyond expression. The journal has continued to thrive and expand under a new manager. This present volume stands as a tribute to all who contributed to the twenty-year existence of *Blueline* and as a promise for the future.

Anthony O. Tyler

Blue Whimsy

Blueline began as no magazine should, without plan beyond the first issue, without marketing research, without financial backers. Compare this with the newest journal focusing on the region, the *Adirondack Explorer,* which spent over five years in preparation before the first issue was launched. *Blueline* was conceived on a whim—its first editors were members of a class on English composition taught by Alice Gilborn at the Arts Center in Blue Mountain Lake; its first subscribers were unwitting guests at a party given by the Gilborns in August 1979. *Blueline*'s one strong point was the idea behind it, an idea that endures to this day—to discover, encourage, and provide a vehicle for Adirondack literature. Later we changed that to "literature dedicated to the spirit of the Adirondacks." Only a few journals were publishing the region's writing then, and those were on the edges of the Adirondacks, not central as we were.

Naming the magazine was easy. Not only did the name clearly identify it with the region, the imaginary line defining the Adirondack Park, but it also carried additional weight as a reference to a printer's proof. In a stretch, it alluded to ice hockey, a typically northern occupation; connotations being our stock and trade, the more we could make of our name, the better. The first issue appeared in the fall of 1979, less than fifty pages, typed by a friend, composed mainly of writings by the composition class with a few poems by reputable and willing regional poets. On the basis of its success, we risked a second issue the spring of 1980, this one more sophisticated because it was printed professionally. We actually published material by people we didn't know. That issue depleted our budget. But as submissions began to flow in, subscriptions followed, a trickle to be sure, but enough to keep us going.

The next year or two became a crash course in the business of small press publishing. In the 1980s, few of us had access to a fax or a computer, and if we did, we didn't know how to use them. Everything—manuscripts, invoices, correspondence, volumes of correspondence—was typed on an old but reliable Smith Corona and sent not by e-mail but by the post office. Although typos abounded, nothing succumbed to fatal error or disappeared into electronic oblivion. Joe Bruchac's *How to Start and Sustain a Literary Magazine* became our mantra. We discovered a new world, the small press network, where we listed and indexed ourselves freely. We seldom had enough money to advertise. We learned that copyright came from the Library of Congress, multiple forms from the New York State tax department, and that libraries required purchase orders. Our local postmistress volunteered to help bundle each issue into zip code destinations so we could pay the lowest mailing rate. We applied for and were presented with an ISSN, a badge of recognition, and essential to the sale and distribution of any journal. We thought of becoming nonprofit but didn't want to fuss with bylaws or a lawyer's fee. At one point we were given a small grant from *Poets and Writers* and, more than once, a financial boost from an enthusiastic subscriber. But each issue always begged the question, would there be another? Yet there was another, and then another, until we had seventeen issues under our belt and a niche in the small press world.

Almost from the beginning, the magazine began to change. The second issue was typeset. Typography depended on the typesetter, and it was never quite the same from issue to issue. We added line drawings to the third issue;

later Potsdam would introduce photographs. In the fall of 1984 we went to a larger trim size, and in 1987 from two issues a year to a double annual issue. One or two issues we promoted as special "theme" issues; once we awarded a prize for the best short story. Our first issue was forty pages; our last from Blue Mountain Lake, 120 pages.

Curiously, when the time seemed right to relocate *Blueline,* it was not for financial reasons. Its Blue Mountain Lake editors simply ran out of wind—none of us could give the magazine the attention it now demanded. By the time one issue was printed—and more than once it would languish at the printer's while we scrambled to assure contributors and subscribers that yes, indeed, we were still in business—and then mailed and distributed to various outlets around the park (usually general stores or drugstores, less often bookstores), it was time to begin the editorial process for the next. Despite the lack of a marketing plan, *Blueline* had earned a modest reputation, and as the quality of submissions steadily improved, their numbers increased. Poems from all over the United States arrived in droves, each poet requiring an answer and sometimes a critique, and individual responses typed painstakingly on the Smith Corona were no longer possible. Meeting twice a month, our dedicated editorial staff read, reacted, sifted, and threw almost everything in the "maybe" pile, which meant repeating the whole performance over again. It was thrilling to receive a poem that was an unmistakable "yes," discouraging to read a story with promise but with no time for the author to revise.

After publication of the 1988 issue and a bit of soul searching, it became clear that we had two choices: abandon *Blueline* to a not-so-early death for literary magazines (we were already in our tenth year), just as the magazine was flourishing, or find some willing, if misguided, institution better equipped to take over our myriad responsibilities. That fall I had a curious lunch with Tony Tyler, chairman of the Potsdam English department, Marlene Youmans, a faculty member whose poems had appeared in *Blueline,* and the dean of Arts and Sciences, whose conversation consisted of polite but pointed queries about why in the world would Potsdam want to venture onto such financial quicksand as a literary magazine? There must have been some interesting memos exchanged at Potsdam that winter. Because in the summer of 1989, still another issue of *Blueline* appeared, bearing the copyright English Department, Potsdam College of the State University of New York. It was with mixed feelings— pride, regret, gratitude—that I tore open the envelope and held the magazine in my hands. At least half of our old contributors had followed *Blueline* to its new home. But something was different; instead of the usual solid color cover was black and white photograph of a rock in the middle of a stream. It looked exactly right.

Alice Wolf Gilborn

Reading *Blueline*

My association with *Blueline* began one day in the spring of 1988 when Tony Tyler and I drove to Blue Mountain Lake to meet with founding editor Alice Gilborn. Alice was anxious to determine that we could successfully continue what she had so lovingly created. I wondered myself what we were undertaking, but as a member of a local Southern writers discussion group, I thought a new literary activity might be fun. Even though I had worked mostly with drama and poetry as a critic and translator (from the Spanish), my interest in *Blueline* was to edit the fiction. Tony, who was primarily interested in poetry, assured me I could be fiction editor. For much of the first five years of producing *Blueline* at SUNY-Potsdam, I also did the layout and whatever else was needed. Gradually, we gathered a group of faculty who shared in making the transition a success.

Reading fiction has always been one of my great joys in life. I did not anticipate the variety of submissions we would receive and naively thought that I would be choosing among Pulitzer Prize caliber stories. Although anxious at first to have enough fiction to meet our standards, I soon realized that would not be a problem and we could achieve the quality we had envisioned that day of the meeting with Alice. It was interesting for me to note that for no reason we could determine the quantity of fiction and poetry submitted from year to year varied significantly. Also, we would receive a number of stories on the same topic in certain years but not in others, for example, fishing, death, garage sales. My *Blueline* years were well spent. Now that I have retired from the modern language department, as well as from *Blueline,* I look back fondly to my collaboration with colleagues in putting out the journal each year. I am sure the current editors, some old and some new, will keep *Blueline* thriving in the twenty-first century.

Myra Gann

Why *Blueline* Isn't Only Blue

"A poet does not work by square or line," said poet William Cowper in "Conversations." Not even when the line is blue, I would add. Not even when that blue line marks the boundary of a magical six-million-acre expanse of forest, mountain, river, and valley called the Adirondack Park.

Poets work by feelings, by dreams, by rhythms, by memories and visions, by voices and pictures swirling inside their heads, I think. And so *Blueline,* the magazine, has tried to be more than just a place for poems and stories and artwork about the Adirondacks. *Blueline* has tried to be a magazine that celebrates more than geography—as grand as that geography is. To me, what it celebrates best is a way of being in the world, a way of looking at the world. And that being and that looking still take account of nature; still respond to its rhythms, its power, its civilizing or corrupting influence. No one has to acknowledge the beauty of nature to appear in *Blueline,* but no one can afford to ignore nature either.

And because all of us are animal and vegetable and mineral, this focus is not unnatural at all. Each of us, in both real and metaphoric ways, is like the Adirondack Park: made up of places forever wild, and places barely civilized, and places full of social density. We have our public zones and our private ones. And in the great social and biological geography of our brains, there are human and animal voices calling out to us.

So this, to me, is what *Blueline* seeks to do in its fiction and its poetry and art: be the occasion, if not the place, where writers and readers who still believe that human lives are inextricably bound up with the forces of nature can find a comfortable place to gather or be.

Alan Steinberg

Lines

Serving as editor of a regional literary journal came as something as a surprise. In the spring of 1998, Tony Tyler was ready to step down as editor and asked if I would be willing to take his place. I admit, I hesitated. I had never subscribed to an aesthetic that was bound by place (or time). Nor did I have what Jim Gould has called the "residency requirement" for writers (and editors?) of the region. It wasn't that I was particularly against the Adirondacks—indeed, I've spend much of my life hovering outside the blue line, slipping across the line to hike or climb, but I had never lived the Adirondack life. Nor was I against the notion of regions—any number of literary journals have redefined themselves by region in recent years and have had startling success in doing so. The question in my mind was whether I had enough interest and the experience to judge a poem or story about Blue Mountain Lake or the High Peaks.

What convinced me that I did have the interest and experience was what had become the journal's subtitle: "a literary magazine dedicated to the spirit of the Adirondacks," or as it is sometimes advertised in calls for submissions: "the shaping influence of nature." Alice Gilborn's essay on Adirondack porches is dead on, and gives an essential understanding of a scene in Jennifer Magnani's "The McDougall Girl"—but in both cases, the porch and its interplay with what is public and private and how we make such distinctions transcends the particular porches in question. Similarly with Kurt Rheinheimer's "Pond" and its representation of the deep social constraints upon our relationships with nature and the delicate interplay between transgression and rejuvenation. These constraints are everywhere particular to a place so completely "managed" as the Adirondack Park, but they also resonate outside the blue line. If there is a residency requirement, it is a residency that transcends space and time.

The lines created by the "spirit" are also more communal than spatial. They are defined by a set of ideas, concerns, and interests and result in a conversation that I feel privileged to overhear. It is also a privilege to help foster that conversation.

Rick Henry

Poetry

Coming to Treeline

I remember the Range
and bushwhacking as a girl
up the side of Mt. Haystack,
scrabbling up trails through thick stands of Fir,
pushing past short, precise pine trees
which politely snapped back into place,
then swishing through the soft forests of Balsam—
those tiny green dwarves waving their whiskbrooms
of sweet incense into thin air,

and finally coming to treeline

first, there is nothing but bracken,
scrub pine and Lapland Sandwort,
but then the skyscraper
of gray granite, looming to the top.

At treeline, all complexity
falls away
and you can see clear
to the blue line
of beyond.

Nearing fifty, I come
to a treeline of my own
and sigh with relief.

Just maybe, I can find
my bearings
now.

Blueline 21 (2000)

PAUL CORRIGAN

Two in an Old Canoe
for Jan

Between us and the lake
it stretches its canvas hide
caulked with tar and bruised
like a fighter's jaw
but smooth as a loon
when, free of the land, it glides
to the squaretail's lair.
Tonight the hungry lunkers
smashed our hackled coachmen,
fooled by the lively dance
of lifeless feathers.
We are fooled by the wide spaces
that hardly hold a ripple,
thinking we're safe from sudden wind
in this tipsy old boat
fashioned from frail cedar ribs
and meant for travel by those
now dead or too feeble
to be of use with a paddle.
I think of all the fishing we do
for words to describe our drifting lives,
words that must fill the space
of our crossing between two shores.
Patched and battered as they are,
we hope their frail design
will keep us afloat, that the wake
they leave behind will ripple
with grace on the wide waters
of the world, that we will
always rise like fish
to the bright feathers of desire.

Blueline 5, no. 2 (1984)

Raspberrying with My Mother

Her tin is brimming with berries
as it did when she was young
and I would pick berries beside her, paying
the price in berries for her pies.
Each July these fields supply her larder
but they are growing back to woods
and she must search among the firs
and birch that crowd the brambles out
to fill her peanut butter pail.
And so she does, quick as ever,
flicking berries into bright containers,
lightly squeezing each with thumb and finger
the way she holds her beads at mass
hoarding prayer as if it were ripe fruit
to be used later in a pie.
But I prefer to eat my pickings.
I crave the wild taste of fresh raspberries,
the soft fuzz that grazes the lips,
the tiny seeds that catch between the teeth.
Like a young bear I gorge myself
on tart gobs of tongue-staining fruit,
growing groggy on the excess
till the thought of dozing off
is more delicious than the pie
I'll get for gathering six cups.
But her sweet tooth takes her beyond this field
and she keeps seeing pies and tarts
and muffins rising in some oven,
lining some pantry shelf. She conjures them
from thin air like a mystic vision
to coax me into building up my stores.
"Are you here to pick or play
my son?" she'll say. And I admit
I share her taste for those unearthly things
like pies and shortcake or a bowl
with milk or cream and freshly gathered berries.

But I must come to some things on my own.
So when the crop is red and full
and falling off the branch, I look
no further than this berry patch
and, like some wild, woods-bred creature,
take only what I find next to my nose.

Blueline 3, no. 1 (1981)

Dipping Smelt

With each pass of the net downstream
the river telegraphs
its restless message through my arms.
Melting snow oozes from its mouth
like words from the wandering mind
of a drunk while the frowning moon
lifts its round face high above us
in disdain. But the moon should know
that soon, before it sinks below the pines,
the river will wax eloquent.
Quick syllables of fish will flash
and writhe in my mesh as it drips
up onto the bank. My next pass
grates against the bottom gravel
but still no fish. I gather only
dripping darkness from the riled waters.
But I plan on netting smelt tonight.
I've plunged through half a mile
of crusty old spring snow
that couldn't hold a bird much less
the load I toted: the skillet,
the lard, the corn meal and the beer.
These fish swim through my mind so often
my thoughts have all become bright fingerlings
and migrated upriver, leaving me
to follow wordless, diminished
by my pursuit of the river's

unseen multitudes. Unlike me,
they're not confused by April's snow-covered
crocuses. They move with the moon,
bringing new life to this artery
of water. They are a sign that soothes me
in this in-between time when I gain
little from putting words on a page,
when I'd do better to glean the riffles,
scooping the schools of silver fry
into my nylon net, straining
the river's darkness till only
their bright living light remains.

Blueline 2, no. 2 (1981)

The Poem as a Valuable Fur Bearing Animal

It is most active after dark
but daytime sightings are common
on the northern slopes of ridges
where the evergreens are thickest.
A strong climber, it moves with grace
through the treetops, overtaking
its prey with a few well-timed leaps.
There is little the poem won't eat:
beetles, bullheads or bass;
grouse, grubs or wild grapes;
anything that doesn't eat the poem first.
It has even been known to steal trout
from the creel of a sleeping fisherman,
to rob milk from the udders of deer.

Look for it near running water.
It likes to dabble for minnows
late in the afternoon when the shadows
hide it from its larger cousin,
the novel, who would gladly make a meal
out of it. Though once very rare,

this shy creature has been reintroduced
over much of its former range.
Teams of trained scientists
have been live-trapping the poem for study,
recording its sex, weight and age
and placing a tag in each ear
before setting it free. Heavily trapped
at the turn of the century
when its soft, thickly matted fur
was in high demand for women's handmuffs
and as a lining for men's galoshes,
the poem is making a comeback
now that its pelt is no longer in vogue.

Blueline 4, no. 1 (1982)

Balance

Where cattails float
redwinged blackbirds swing
on disappearing light.
A pond called Round
full of lilies, frog song—
green against waxy petals white—
those liquid eyes flash
into dark waters blind.

By touch and tap, the water
eases back into itself.
Dull heat and bug noise
whirring—
I take memory of this life:
the hard grit that remains
in bony shells—
the hour the heron
bends to its small fish.

Blueline 12 (1991)

TONY COSIER

Wild Strawberries

Studying feathery snowlines of crystals over shadow
On a day so cold even the rock seems frozen,
We find tucked away the familiar sawtoothed edge
Of the tiny triple leaf.

We've seen them run green in November,
Prolific in places they'll be
When the first soft mud comes slushing,
Back to the air in spring.

In flowering time,
Their white and gold array
Will blaze in patches so thick
We'll be pressed to find a spot to place a foot.

Meadow creepers, they will storm hills if inclined,
Dive deep woods, percolate tall grass
Huddled so low you can find them after mowing
Still deftly succulent red under leaf.

They are wild, will not be cropped,
Mischievously keep berries nothing but minuscule
That no one could hoard in a bowl,
Self-willed, fragile, too delicate almost to taste,

Except by the few who love them enough
To become like them. Patient. Subtle. Willing to
Dip small centered; concentrate;
Cherish the elixir, bear the stain.

Blueline 14 (1993)

Wild Apples

We knew them first by a redness in the bark,
The way they had of splaying from the trunk,
Then ovate leaves and nubbing twigs, and wind dance, each flower
A pink haze flushing through a five-pointed bed of white;

At last, the fruit rounding and riding profusely
Through thicket and hedge and fenceside, everywhere we looked,
Wanton in clusters. Apples twisted at eye level
And scattered abundant. Some grew heavy and thumped to grass.

Hundreds bubbled skyward out of reach.
Always a firm coquettish few at handstretch
Demanded a touch of fondling in the plucking,
A curve of the flesh to the applecurve before they would give.

Yellow or green or russet cornered, they leaned to tartness.
Even when bagged, they held to feistiness.
A ripple as light as a hand's through water
Would thunder them softly like vanishing hooves of deer.

Cut, submerged, and boiled, they keep their odor.
Their mash and scum stay applelike. Their warm and subtle
Thread of steam burgeon full of quality.
As the spooned mass thickens to a pendant globe,

It centers and pulls at something deep in us.
Tomorrow we will pick from a tree a little
Farther out where nature is taking more
Of the pasture back a little faster. The next
Day after that, we'll forage deeper still.

Blueline 16 (1995)

After Finding a Photo of Kensett's *Lake George, 1858* in the Paper

His painting of the lake named
for a king—time folds
back to this summer, our walk
among the Revolution cannon and redoubts,
then the village where tourists crowd
at doors of restaurants and shops,
and parasails towed by motorboats lift
over the water to shape
like ancient, perfect clouds.

Not far—Prospect Mountain.
Ascending, we look over
the Narrows, the Eagle's Eye, a busload
of prisoners working to cut back
that wild growth by our highway.
Mother tells us she and my father
in the thirties hiked all the way—
hours up a dirt trail
to the lookout tower. We drive
almost to the summit, park
in a huge, paved lot, but choose
not to ride the viewmobile, with its guide
and amplified music. Instead, we climb, finally
come out from the trees to worn-smooth rock
that holds now only the base of the tower,
the rest of the structure gone—
but our view still finding the lake
and range after range of preserved wilderness,
from this height still close
to Kensett, and to that time of the king
who never came to see it.

Blueline 12 (1991)

Nightfall

The wood begins to gather darkness,
stuffing it in holes
and spreading it in hollows,
tucking it among the tree roots,
piling it against the sapling's trunk.
At first the upper branches stay aloof
preferring not to watch
the hoarding going on below,
but darkness stacks on darkness
stacks on darkness, up and up,
until the glutton woodland
vanishes from sight,
itself consumed in blackest night.

Blueline 16 (1995)

JOHN GREY

The Clock Stops

When it's winter
it's as if it's always been winter,
as if the wind only knows
to blow from the North.
Snow-smothered trees stand motionless,
have no history.
The fields are blank.
The sky, a droll blue joke
with a scattering of joyless birds.

Through a season of staring,
I'm convinced there is no green,
that the landscape is always this
somber, this still,
that the limbs, when exposed,
will be bare as the sunlight,
that we will never move on
from this time,
that what drably melts on the edges
of the roof, of the sill,
is the next moment
bored with waiting
and now, never to be.

Blueline 19 (1998)

A Woman Out on the Lake Is Singing

A woman out on the lake is singing,
alone her oars touching
and letting go, a woman in a boat
is singing. She is going down the arm
at dusk, singing, on the lake, a woman,
alone. I lean out over the shore, see light catch
in the lake dripping from her oars,
Alone, she's fading between water
and sky singing, a tone
that forgives us all.

Blueline 11 (1990)

On Schroon River at 40

I had grown used to
the silence.
Nothing between us.
Father.   Son.
Always felt it.
Penny pressed to the tongue.
Bitter. Cold. Corrosive.

But this morning
the silence fills up,
the way our canoe fills
with August light,
me at the helm, you the stern,
steering us, navigating us
around downed branches
that snag this bolt of black silk
God shook out between mountains.

As we paddle without a word,
beating a hollow,
ghostly drumming
on the boat's sides,
I imagine
Iroquois braves returning
to Schroon's summer shores,
or perhaps fur traders,
their canoe plush with pelts
trapped up-river.
Other, long-ago fathers and sons
filling their own silences,
paddling this ancient stream of solace:

I can grow used to
this silence
between us.

Blueline 20 (1999)

From Winslow Homer's Notebook: *Frog on Mink Pond, 1891*

Still as stone, brown as mud
that shores the pond,

green mouth sinister set
about some bug, or its memory,

just as sinister set,
this time on me,
eyes black with coronal gold.

Once, just before he spotted me,
a final foghorn note,
jowls ballooning around what words
frogs will say.

Now alert
ears flat to his flat head
clash like silent cymbals
against the air
with my slightest stir:

As my brush washes across the page
our hearts beat. But for different reasons,
his from fright, mine from delight.

Blueline 10 (1989)

Memorial Day Parade

Our boy balances
his drum between bony knees.
He marches down Main Street
closer to us now,
eyes straight ahead seeing
neither me, left,
nor you, right.
He marches toward the tombstones;
he livens what is dead.

In our kitchen, no, mine,
this wet dawn
I fixed rice pudding:
stirred sugar and rice, some cinnamon and vanilla
into two quarts of oldish milk,
poured it into the cracked brown bowl,
set it in the oven to thicken
long and slow.
It's baking now, its rice swelling, milk hardening,
cream densing down to bride-white velvet.

Our boy is closer now.
His muffled beats keep time.

If you were home now,
you could think cinnamon-thoughts, in drifts.
They'd make you smile
long and slow.
Make you want to taste warm velvet,
soothe your parched lips,
bathe your tongue, cleanse my palate.
It's smooth as silk, delicious really,
made from almost-sour milk.

The rain will end this afternoon,
bring gnats and knots
of before we were deafened by rhythmic drums,
caught up in marching to tombstones,
honoring what is dead.

He's here, now hear.
Light stabs through swift clouds.
You squint against the sun.
I watch you sight our boy:
Our drummer pounds, incensed he beats
this requiem for the dead.

Come home,
I want to say across Main Street.
I've made a nice rice-pudding
from almost-sour milk.

Blueline 16 (1995)

JAN ZLOTNIK SCHMIDT

A Corot Landscape

yellow light weaves in and out
of fanned edges
of spruce and poplar and locust
meadows rise in green
a thick seeping like sea grass

the only sounds
the fitful stirrings
of night breezes
and fireflies
the fitful ravaging
of children foraging for light.

Blueline 12 (1991)

Flowering Dogwood

Oval, silvery foliage
that seems to float above the trunk
in a feathered illusion
of shape, tier after tier
of precise leaves,
deeply veined, and reddish
twigs, pithy limbs,
tight clusters of abundant,
purpled fruit.

Walking out to the edge
of the cultivated fields
early this morning,
wondering again where
the name dogwood first began:
from the dense muscle
of the heartwood
of the gruff bark,
persistent roots perhaps,
the fiercely loyal,
vernal blooms?

Blueline 12 (1991)

The Least of Things

This is not something I've made up.
Not entirely. One can see the signs of things broken,
partially undone. The least of things.
As if we arose to a time in which we had no memories to relate,
no language sufficient to touch them,
no glistening berries dropping to the ground.
Not yet. No ripe persimmons, no rose hips.
No untold beauty and its fruit nearby.

But factored into the landscape anyway,
like the rain, the sunlight, the rock.
Like the wild wind that rises from nothing and nowhere
and just as suddenly and completely disappears.
Unseen, unremarked, unwritten. This,
then. A parsimony, a carrying only
of the essential. The fallen leaf
picked up, carried away. But somehow
remembered and repeated.
A presence on the leaf scar of the twig.
What was. The only thing we know.

Blueline 21 (2000)

Sleight of Hand

It's so quiet you can hear
snow fill the meadow
and stillness gather steam.

Trees float like islands
in the sound
as horses turn from earth to sky.

If not for these tracks
forgetting their place
every direction would be the same.

You would disappear.

Blueline 18 (1997)

Gray

The color of Lake Placid.

The water with which I wash away the pain of seven summers.

The cold waves of the big lake.

The smooth waters of smaller Mirror Lake.

Whiteface on a stormy day before it deepens to black as the mountain disappears after sundown.

Mother's eyes hardening into agate stones.

The Lake Placid Skating Arena where Mother sits in the stands warm in her mink coat and stadium boots, angry as she watches Nanette, my sister, struggle on the ice.

The days of rain in August when I run to the Public Library to read the children's books, then the adult ones, until I read them all.

The Hollywood stars that make Peggy and me laugh and cry at the Lake Placid Cinema: Shirley Temple and Spring Byington, Bing Crosby and Barry Fitzgerald, Clark Gable and Claudette Colbert.

The limousines of the wealthy camp owners who send their chauffeurs and maids to do the marketing at Shea's grocery store.

The charcoal portrait I make of my sister, transforming her into a twisted decayed tree that can never bear leaves.

Gus Lussi, the exclusive teaching pro, and his elegant tweed jacket, Tyrolean cap and baton, which he holds off the ice for his protégés to leap over as they practice their jumps.

The sharks that I imagine under the ice, lying in wait to devour me.

The airmail stationery Peggy keeps so carefully to write long letters to her family in Scotland.

Peggy's white hair that she rinses with blueing every few weeks.

The Olympic Arena, with romanesque arches at each end, where every skater prays for triumph.

The shadow cast as I fall again and again on the cold ice.

Blueline 20 (1999)

Freeze

It is time: For two days I watch;
Although always, every year, I suppose,
I will be surprised, unprepared.
The night before, the lake was rippled black
And cold as crows' caws, with raven tracery
Of willow and birch, dark against the twilight.

The next morning wind could not move
Blackened water, crystalled and tense.
The ice held by thinnest magic,
For I knew the first touch of morning sun
Would dispel webs floating like smoke
Above dark stones and deep fish
Fanning translucent fins
In the center of the lake.

No sun all day, and the webs pushed
Open water to the center of the lake.

Last night I dreamt of my father:
He visited me from his deep death,
His face contorted with the need
To tell me something he had forgotten.
His hair floated in front of his round, white eyes,
And he brushed it away with vague fingers;
His lips writhed, but I heard nothing.

This morning ice is gray and stiff.
During the shuttered night, snow fell
And thickened trees, ground, water.
Snow lies on the hard, new ice
And disappears as it falls, spinning,
In the water in the center of the lake.

Blueline 19 (1998)

ROGER MITCHELL

Reuben Sanford and John Richards, Surveyors, Make Their Report, October 1827

" . . . where an ordinary surveyor could hardly be
paid for the exercise of his profession."
                              —Charles Fenno Hoffman

" . . . the desart place where we were."
                              —Peter Kalm

The most easterly line of this tract
is also on land of second quality,
the term, first, being inappropriate
to any we saw in all those weeks.
From the southeast corner to the river,
it is fifty-five chains. Thence,
on very rough steep hills and high mountains,
rocky, and the passage thwarted
on all sides by fallen trees, mossed,
and of great size and age, their criss-
crossing of one another so continual
and inveterate as to be often vexatious.
This is of fourth quality, no more,
where streams and twisted brooks rush down
between the rocks and mountains,
leaving no smooth place anywhere.
One hill or mountain crowds close behind
the other all along, reaching,
at the north boundary and on rough steep hills
a very high rocky spruce-bound mountain.
The land, we repeat, is of the worst kind,
but for a few small pieces to the south.
On the west, it is again rocky, broken,
though timbered with spruce, cedar, fir,
some beech and a multitude of birch.
Stupendous rocks and ledges, craggy
and irregular, in many places

RANDY LEWIS

suddenly there was a loud noise

you were sitting on the bed
reading Edward Abbey
I was lying next to you
reading Raymond Carver
it was late and dark
suddenly there was a loud noise
outside the open window
the garbage can knocked over again
I said maybe a bear this time?
you said I doubt it
I handed you the flashlight
you went into the night
to check it out
and I haven't seen you
since
the cat is meowing
chasing moths that bounce their heads
against the screens
the children are all asleep
it is summer
we are both forty
but not for long.
please come back.
we're just getting
to the good part.

Blueline 17 (1996)

Up Here

I lie down across this fault line, across
twinned crystals and scattered garnet
at the verge of space. Here
I am the negative
of these outcrops, rifts, fissures. I
hug them close and—
cloud splitter—I am the one who
cleaves the sky.

I meet the dark-eyed junco
above the barrens. He takes me
to Chazy Lake and Lyon Mountain,
to lonesome waters, lying alone in the rock.
I kneel and drink. We
dart the fringed gentian, suck its
blue nectar. I am
the bluebead lily, the spreading
starflower, its seven petals.
The white-throated sparrow
eyes me, up here
blooming near treeline.

Blueline 11 (1990)

NOEL SMITH

The Ausable River Not Itself

The drought is in its sixtieth day.
The leaves have gone belly up.
The granite of the river's bed shows.

Right by the falls, pictured on postcards
as a place of bone crushing terror,
the water is running so low

that even babies and grandmothers
can toddle in the teeth of the main
branch and still keep their balance.

Barking boys full of braggadocio
glide their bodies right down the bed
of the main falls yelping and waving

their beer at the place where
three months ago the river sent
chicken coops splintering to the cliff.

A little downstream roared that thundering
chasm the river gouged from granite
Where the tour busses gather in chrome herds.

Today the sign says, "Chasm closed because
of low water." A child says to his mother,
"The river does not want us to see it like this."

Blueline 21 (2000)

MARJORIE MADDOX

Ithaca Winter

To undo who I was, I opened
my chapped lips and swallowed
the weather whole.

Wind chatters grief discriminately,
clicks with the crick in a neck,
the chill in a spine, unzips
eventually what isn't.

Snow fills an eye's iris,
wets the slick of winter,
warms what is without
insides, retrospect burning
its last embers in the grate.

What better white
to white-out absence,
lose the clean slate entirely?

I had a life disappear once.
I stepped out of it into the snow
stacked up like an isosceles triangle
on Seneca Street, and old name and sorrow
stuck at the bottom in a drift.

When I stopped shivering,
behind my teeth were words.

Blueline 20 (1999)

To the Vermont Ferry

In the yellow air
maples hang their laggard leaves,
translucent emblems
of the furbished signs
for autumn house-shops
the aged travelers and I
are lingering in
to finger crafts that have restored
the lakeside prospects,
theater groups and chat.

Vermillion vines
hold trees and walls
in casual readiness
for a brisk wind,
off-lake reminder
of the season's schedule.

We walk about from lunch
and see the choppy boat
arrive: the gravel jetty
has its quota, but we
are duly there and now
are going on
to blocks that keep us all
from rolling off, and stand
toward another shore
another state.

Blueline 22 (2001)

MAURICE KENNY

Eagle

After a Drawing by Kahionhes

In respect . . .
    I draw your name . . .
shadow on shoulder
wing on cheek
feather hanging in my hair.

You hold sky,
touch where my fingers,
or thoughts,
can neither penetrate
nor would dare.

In flight you flame in sun,
burning feathers and eyes,
and in cobalt darkness,
royal and original,
I feel the presence
on each mountain,
each spire of pine
and shiver in that breeze
your wings fan . . .

Knowing I am to stand
with my feet hearing words
in the earth,
and ears
song from the skies,
space touching space
unconceived,

Confident, certain
you and the mountain and pine
will endure
and our grandchildren
draw your name.

Blueline 6, no. 2 (1985)

This is Plenty

I do need to go back and back
through the enormous and minuscule history of beings.
I can start here with this woman and our past.
The floor of the brain is six bones.
We sweep together. We fly on the four wings of the sphenoid,
the great wings, the complex forms
like delicate moths of bone that fly within the skull,
moths behind our eyes
Such discoveries connect us. The eyes show marvels
with weak currents in fluids
as light fixed landscapes for Fox Talbot without drawing
or time spent acquiring a craft.
If I need ancestors, I take a sponge in a shallow sea
in upstate New York, a coral as an old bouquet,
a fish whose mouth opened like a mailbox.

Blueline 20 (1999)

A Cure for Its Crying

When it has cried longer
than you can stand it, try
doing this. Hold it against
your shoulder, pat its back
with a gentle hand, and whisper
to it: There, there . . . there, there.
Forget how late it is, how tired
you are. It could die, crying
too long. It is much like a baby.

Blueline 17 (1996)

Harbinger

When Orion strides upon the western sky,
The dog at heel behind him in the dark,
The slow stars moving on now only mark
How endless the long winter and the night
At last the February morning streaks the east,
Pours slowly among birch trees and the pines,
And stars that fade in silence,
Suddenly are gone where they just shone.

In growing light the woods stand up,
Snow-covered fences, here our drifted bar—
No respite from the sleeping season.
Yet here beside the house
Sometime yesterday
The sun laid a brown-grass
Wedding ring around the elm.

Blueline 12 (1991)

A Lawn Colonized by Orb Spiders

Each white extravagant shield
is macabre lace—like Queen Anne's,
ballasted by a dark blot.

Orb on orb, the seventeen
bounce when the little mistral
of fall blows, as it does always,

and the half-dried flashes of color,
snared geranium heads and leaves,
shake and spindle in the autumn wind.

The orbs are twiddling contraptions—
a leaf acrobat, clamped by cobweb
to a wire, swivels by her teeth,

precarious, daring—mornings one must
sweep from the door the circus
leftovers of afternoon, the big nets

and flying trapeze. After a while
one grows accustomed to the twitter
of performing leaves, one grows sleepy

and closes shutters against the air's
immense curtains of lace. And drifts.
The house dozes, sending forth

a pale cloud-light, a cocoon
fit for a dying star. Now
spiders thicken their white canopies,

spinning in orbits a spherical song.
In the house a dimpled woman slumbers
and dreams that the usual excessive

snow has begun. She battens in the cocoon
of autumn sleep and, menstrual, longs
for a promised child cool as snow.

Blueline 9 (1988)

Boundary Lines

The demarcations of the ancient kings
had holy force. Their rubbled fields
were scored with imperious boundary lines.
Even now, the opaque black
frontier-markers of the Assyrians
—*kudurru* stones, illumined in museums—
peg the imagination to their roots.

Haphazard boundaries intrigue.
When a rock cracks beneath the cold
its cloven symmetries suggest
some partitioned homeland.
The divisions frost designs
on the moist interiors of windowpanes
are chimerical as the adages
prisoners chalk along the walls of cells.
Whatever cuts a world
into arbitrary shards
puzzles and appalls.

And there stand
the wincing boundary lines between
glances and confessions of the hands.
There pace the fiercely sentried
intervals of words:

What I never said
to you alive
lags at the iron boundaries of the dead.
What I didn't give
to you when I could
ends underfoot where all
the voices mob
the margins of our farthest borderposts
in speechless territories, stopped with snow.

Blueline 20 (1999)

Railway Stanzas

I have always found railway stations sad.
The aura of departure lingers there.
The rails that stretch away in parallel,
abraded brightness dismay, like those problems
in your old mathematics books at school;
outmoded, they yet sting the intellect
with formalin conundrums of the time that's left.
I think of all the leavetakings I've known.
Airports are abstract. Railroads have
valedictory fragrances,—the seethe of steam,
a scorched whiff of oil. I think of
lovers waving as the platform fades.

And yet, a hankering for depots, terminals,
is a symptom of good health, a robust mind.
Arrivals also figure in my dreams
where they take on the shape of engine spokes.
I used to see the spokes and wheels as a frieze,
not as an engine but a dark geometry,
tableaux of pistoned possibilities,
without a single ledge for tears,
without the ineluctable hankie of farewells,
the blurred mascara of a momma's eyes,

dad's mustache all atremble, baby's howls,
the structure of forsakenness as the station speeds

out of sight and hearing into memory:
The dainty Edwardian melancholy
of junctions, switching places, water tanks;
the bright red afterthought of the caboose
with men, suspendered, sucking corncob pipes
on the little black-railed platform at the back;
and there was also that sleek smell of rails,
the bitter cloudiness of iron gauge,
the creosote-soaked ties and gouging spikes,
the deferential signal-bars, the throb of the shrill
light. But most, a pale opacity of windows
in a nighttime train, a glimpse of shaded lamps

and diners all embraced in goldenness
and wisps of smoke, the porter leaning between
the sleeper and the observation car, —
watched in a shriek of speed from a trestle by
the slow, muddy river underneath.
And sometimes I had stuck a silver dime
to the outer rail before the train went by
and now retrieved it as the distance took
the companionable apocalypse away:
the coin was faceless now and hammered flat
and it felt hot and smooth and was transformed
in my fingers to a fossil of velocity.

I do not write this from nostalgia.
I who once revered as a mercy of
certitude the benignity of fact
am skeptical of every reverie
that leads me back into dubious time.
A sense of destination, though, beguiles
me still, the piercing and metallic scent
of almost indiscernible adieux.
It is momentum now that holds me, the

quick kiss on the steps, the conductor's
cry, the stirring of the great black wheels
in spires of steam toward their unyielding speed.

Blueline 14 (1993)

Spider Silk

Once, when I gashed my finger Grandmother
led me to the linen closet down the hall.
There towels and bedsheets lay in fragrant folds
and an old, outgrown doll with bright-blink eyes
that scared me with its stiff hilarity
bled sawdust from its mouth onto a shelf.
Grandma pulled me close to her until
I understood the comfort of her touch.
She poked her free hand in the crevices
and spooled a spiderweb around her nails.
She wound the web again around my wound.
She daubed it tenderly until the clots of silk
touched my blood and then my bleeding stopped
almost at once.

There, among the smell of sheets,
in the cold, fresh, dark place that had scared me so,
Grandmother gave me her most secret smile.
Since that day,
learning to love the doubleness of things,
I think the spider silk is in my blood.

Blueline 15 (1994)

Rain

The smell of rain brings back the house we had,
leads me down hallways toward unopened doors,
resurrects the pine smell of its old floors,
seats our dead lost kinfolk in the sad
front sitting-room once more. O the dark rain

tunnels time and brings me back again
to the gray windows where I felt the pain
of being small and unprotected; then
the sense of all outside was distanced by
thunder pommeling the startled trees,
the stropped lightning with its traceries,
while I felt only how the pupil of my eye
fell into the darkness of the room behind
where fear switched out the lamp and drew the blind.

Blueline 15 (1994)

Bee Balm

Their dusty spires of blossoms look washed out,
Topple to the touch, a bone-pale lavender;
But monarchs flutter them, and fat bees
Tumble into their bleak intoxicating blooms.
On August mornings you will find the bees
Half-dead with feeding on the dizzy stems.
They grip their flowers in a love-clutch, feet
Enlaced, their black metallic eyes dulled with balm.
The tall chalky petals drip with bees.
When the sun comes they twitch and shudder awake.
To us the scent is hot and mordant, prompts
Sneezes. To bees it is sweeter than home,
All night they cling sybaritic as pashas,
Their stiff golden fur dampened with pleasure.

Blueline 10 (1989)

Geese at Midnight

an armada of
pewter shapes
moving in darkness,
about to slip
close to shore.
Camouflaged in
shadow, you can't
see anything at
first. Then, the
moon's tongue
licks the only
thing moving on
the skin of water.
They glide through
weeds, the world
of fish below them,
slick and noise-
less, trailing
feathers as
glitter ripples

Blueline 17 (1996)

June on Whiteface

Huddled close, dwarf foliage,
tea of Labrador bursts its spume,
while along the jagged mountain ridge
miniature laurels bloom.
Bunchberry patches hug the ground,
their dogwood blossoms green to white.
Lady slippers, white or pink gowned,
and trillium shelter 'neath hardwoods might.
　　Lofty mountain, rugged spine,
　　Faerie flowers garland this chine.

Blueline 20 (1999)

ALAN STEINBERG

Loon Calls

My heart stops
at the calling,
as if the sound
were older and deeper
than the nerves
that guard my blood.

I cease all conversation
all complaint,
like Job
at a voice from heaven.

At each call
I take heart, take wing,
for all the weight
of my soul,
for all the weight
of my learning.

If ever we could feel
sadness without suffering,
loneliness without pain,
this would be the song
we would sing.

Blueline 10 (1989)

Retreat

I slink into evening's solitude
like a rat among the ruins,
and wear silence
like the river wears the moon.

Light as a shadow on midnight frost,
still as moss on a river bed,
I let time flow
like widows' tears on the dead,

till darkness, like an ancient prophet
heralding some final order,
rises up and
walks on the frozen water.

Blueline 20 (1999)

Naming Creatures

Han-Shan dreamed and walked his Cold Mountain
In the valley and heights of Bunn Hill
In season the door of this old house opens
To children playing naked in the garden
My sons seeking snakes by the creek
A woodchuck crunching the grass
His flesh
Aroused in preying
Ruddy dawn calls
Of a cardinal seeding his mate
While the click clack black brotherhood
Grackles cowbirds redwings
Strut and pluck the lawn
Breaks now fiercely wakened
Wings plumed high
Translating song into moving sight
Quick chickadees dart to the seed
Homers wing homeward
Goldfinches rollercoaster waves of wind
Alert grace in every moment
Deer munch green apples
Under arching trees
Clinging air kisses lingering lovers
Two cats and a Muscovy duck stray my way
Towhee and white-throat dance the hill for food
By chipmunks cheeky with seed
On the ledge glaring inward
Grosbeaks land in abundance
Ululance of foxes in twilight woods
Spring's rabbits near the singing creek
From parallel trees catbirds mock in stereo
My God there in the winter yard
Winged flashes of yellow blue red
Turn snow into a spurting rainbow

Round the feeder and surrounding ground
And Christ three early robins
Feast on flaming tongues of sumac
All to visit me
At home
High on Bunn Hill
Dreaming Han-Shan awake again
In these moments of silent attention

Blueline 2, no. 2 (1981)

ERIC GANSWORTH

Vulnerability

You tell me as we lie in a bed so dark
the moonlight does not even touch
our eyes with a wavering wink
across their liquid surfaces that you are more
than certain when you are in the shower
I will betray you, the warm comforting baptism
removing my lingering influence and you are left
alone with your most secret
thoughts obscure in steam
on slick tiles.

That I have never grown
accustomed enough to showers that I can think
of anything other than the luxury of them
when I am under the water would reveal too much
of who I am and where I have come from
standing naked before a basinful I had pumped
and heated myself making every swipe
of the washcloth count
evaluating my own reflection growing
more vague in the filmy water of my past.

Blueline 20 (1999)

Summer's Dray

The August afternoon
of cicadas, crows,
bee-sweet red-topped clover
soon blends into moonlight
and stars that glint
on woodland harness bells—
snowy tree crickets
guiding a team of shadow horses
as they pull sunflower summer
one more day toward fall.

Blueline 13 (1992)

winter walk to schuyler lake
for Jay

in the harsh socket of the year
we walk through corn stubble,
hoist tattered stalks,
into the wind.

last summer's celebrations
squawk like foraging crows.
ignoring us,
they dip and rise among uneven rows.

water filled and frozen,
the road's deep tractor gullies,
tripping us,
form opaque patterned traps.

i tap the white ice
with my boot toe to hear the thick
clip of water breaking.
the lake reclines before us. a line

of trees curves toward the shore.
and here is surface—
earth's white flat cheek
offered to winter sky.

the calligraphy of crow wings
and the cracked scorn
of their aerial sawing joy
challenge me.

i step onto the waves.
their stiff formality
lifts me above sleeping
fish, the graves and eggs

of next year's dragonflies.
be careful you call, don't drown.
i pound the surface like a drum
and cry aloud, to show you

despite the winter dangers
of our lives, how very safe
we must pretend
to be.

Blueline 10 (1989)

Blood Root

I have seen
a light green
leaf, closely
coiled around
a stalk, emerge
through winter
brown leaves.

A flower rose
above, white
as fresh snow
atop a mountain.

Eight oval petals
opened like
parts of an eye
eager to behold
all that's new.

I dug and scratched
the rootstock
and saw a red
juice out of which
Patowatami boiled
tea to bathe burns
and settlers squeezed
onto a lump of sugar
they held in the mouth
to cure sore throat.

White petals,
open again beneath
my eyelids.

Leathery leaves,
rub against
my fingertips.
Red potion,
cure this tongue
and move it
toward praise
of your powers.

Blueline 21 (2000)

Places

My ancestors worked
hired hands in fields along a river;

others worked on boats
carrying cargo downstream.

I was born and grew up
inland in the hills.

I have lived as an adult
on a fish-shaped island

and I shall return
deep into woods

in which spirits rise
like spring water

and meander downhill
over sandstone.

Blueline 22 (2001)

MATTHEW J. SPIRENG

Hay Mowed and Raked

Hay mowed and raked in low windrows lies dried
on a day of blue sky, of sun so bright
each view seems frozen in crystalline light.
Slow waves roll across high grass on a wide

field rising uncut out beyond that mowed
as a light wind blows from the north and west.
And almost beyond sound a tractor crests
a hill with bailer and wagon in tow,

slowly rolling along a windrow. There,
squared and bound, hay is hurled up by machine
in a high parabola where it seems
to float forever, held only by air.

Blueline 16 (1995)

Queen Anne's Lace

Gathering what's simple and there
all around is child's play. They see
what we don't in stones and fill their
pockets with weight we'd soon as not

bear. They watch ants by the hour
crossing the lawn where we would walk
unmindful of the lives our
feet crush out. They pick dandelions

gone to seed by the score, blow pale
parachutes in the air until
it seems a snowstorm's there. The pail
at the beach is filled with the same

small shells we curse as we walk to
the water. They gather Queen Anne's
Lace until we tell them it's too
much. They point to the heart in each.

Blueline 13 (1992)

Four-Leaf Clover

It isn't luck so much as
persistence, searching
through roadside growth,
the pink-and-white clover bolls
and all that green, the leaves
overlapping so you'd think
every other had an extra leaf,
the honey bees gathering and
that air, clear as light
in August. It's luck no bee stings
your bared arms, your hands dipping in
spreading leaves to find
just one mutant stem
to pick and keep.

Blueline 14 (1993)

Patterns

There is the delicacy of ferns,
curled fiddleheads emerging
in the understory of tall oak woods,
the touch of green that lingers
long past fall's first frost,
the pattern of fronds etched
when winter comes on windows'
lower panes, melting where
children's hands press warmth
under fingers' whorls, losing
form where letters, words appear.

Blueline 22 (2001)

NEAL BURDICK

Waiting for a Train at the Plattsburgh Amtrak Station

A stray
perhaps a cat
has left its mark
upon
a dark green
door that used to open
to a spacious room
where
my father told me
men in derby hats
smoked cigars and sent
commodities
to shining city markets
It's been locked up firmly now for
forty years or more

Lake Champlain slaps gray
and dirty foam on rocks
past rows of rusted tracks
where Plattsburgh put a sewage plant
about the time the railroad yard shut down

Misty drizzle nearly
snow
makes the single track
that still gets used with any regularity
reflect as though it had been polished by
some long-dead Casey Jones
who took a kind of pride
we can't imagine now
in nearly living locomotives
under his command

Wind gusts whirlpool
cigarette butts and candy wrappers
torn remnants of last fall's leaves
across the blacktopped station platform
as dull brick towers
shingled turrets
tombstones to Victorian
exuberance
drip rain and melting snow

The fancy logo "D&H"
initials of the company that
ran this line a century and some
before a huge Canadian conglomerate stepped in
protrudes
from plywood shields
far up the streetside wall
a bit less blue and gold with
every passing year

The waiting room
a former trackside storage space
contains a pair of scarred-up wooden benches
rescued when they
turned the grand old lobby
into a restaurant
that didn't last
a rack with Amtrak schedules to
places few from here will ever go by train
two chain-smoking college kids
a clock that ticks
and ticks
and ticks
to the rhythm of the icy rain

Blueline 22 (2001)

A Dream of Silver

at Mogollon
Geronimo's earth was turned
for silver money

now gashed white slag
falls in a river of bone

crenellated tin buildings rust
battle clashing
wind corrugated
fading daguerreotypes

I found one log house
with a bare electric bulb
hanging from a low logged ceiling
useless as a desert sluice box

a bad toothed old man
said he was a miner
worked this very mountain
forty years and more

I asked him what he had found
in the earth
spending all that time
huddled in the dark below

he guffawed and
said the silver dollars
had rolled away

now the dinosaur bones
lay scattered and unburied
the only ceremony for them
is the mountain limping back

Blueline 3, no. 1 (1981)

YVETTE A. SCHNOEKER-SHORB

Birds and Atoms

Once she leaves her shell,
the vulture knows
those zones of orbits
closest to the earth,
that grounding nucleus,
are filled
with the motion of other birds,
so she seeks the bluest
layer of flight spectrum.

Like an energized electron
circling the edge
of some outermost orbital,
she waits to interact
with the gods
or at least be pulled
to the invisible heavens
of a less negatively charged
other world.

But she never crosses
the spheres,
for there is no ionic bridge,
and no covalent sharing
of her and another,
to bond the two worlds.
Even with all that energy,
her release is still
a downward spiral.

Birds and atoms,
vultures and electrons—
everything is motion;
when the wings

complete the final flap,
atoms untrap
themselves from each cell,
electrons flying
to more attractive forms.

Blueline 16 (1995)

The Error of Light

A bushel of apples, two barefoot women
on the downstairs porch. Fruit turns
against angled knives, cowbells
off-key from the far pasture keep time
quiet. Upstairs
bootsteps heavy on the floorboards,
a shifting of weight, of the hour.

Beyond the barn, trees crowd
closer. Foxes haunt the dense places
green has vanished, grey
the only shade this hour knows.

The women work in tandem
and in silence. Shapes spread
indistinct and none can trace
outlines, shifting ground,
how soap froth on porcelain
loses its name.

The younger one considers
apple flesh, crisping green and sweet.
She chews and swallows, eats
thoroughly and without blinking.
The elder, rocking, shuts her eyes,
recalls each one
who sparked or slashed her faith
unknowing, reminding of the doggedness
of trees.

          Face to the mist,
she rises, blends back in leafy dark,
and turns the corner
alone. The younger, startled, dribbles

juicy words, the tough ones
curl like parings to the wooden floor.

Blueline 10 (1989)

Still in November, Trout

Brightness and a touch of chill hone
all the edges, trees jump
against deep sky.
You cast down into a shiver of stars,
wind and sunlight on the water.

Beneath my feet, riverstones magnified
past clarity, shapes on the creekbed
more secret than silted water.
Tangled moss on the bank whispers
the way to old marshes, sighs
of damp growing things fading.
In the shallows, cattails
chant to music not yet written, fast-
moving water hums one strong note,
I hear your call
rolling. I slide back
into the cool river, arc
with the current, swimming
in the deep of your voice.

Blueline 10 (1989)

Fish's Car

It was as gray as a bullet
before we painted it Canary Yellow
in celebration of its 300,000th mile.
1977 Buick LeSabre
fast as a bullet, too,
thirty-four tickets
in twelve states and two Canadian Provinces
to prove it.
Eight hot cylinders gulping
fuel like iced tea,
two hub caps, driver's side only,
a stuffed ferret baring teeth
on the back dash
with purple, orange, red, and blue
Mardi Gras beads around its neck,
a cassette deck that only played
Aretha Franklin,
and a hood ornament that could have been
Bo Derek complete with a Canary Yellow
string bikini
thanks to Dan Jette's steady hand.
Each ride in Fish's car
was my last:
power steering gone since '87,
tires as bald as baloney,
and Fish's impatience
which always made him pass.
I never cared:
If that car was going to heaven,
I wanted to ride the whole way.

Blueline 19 (1998)

J. L. KUBICEK

Peeking

Who has not been drawn—
entranced by
the waving threads
of web and wing—
spider and dragonfly?
Such delicacy
was created, surely,
by the master
on the day of rest,
to catch
and hold light
in veiled dance
and in your peeking . . .
witness being.

Blueline 19 (1998)

One Year

The rough-legged hawk
returns down the ridges from
the north. A single leaf cuts
loosely through the west wind
as the golden birches grapple
blue sky. Everything
hurries somewhere even
as we stop & build this rest.
A woodpecker stalks the barn-wall.
Crowns of red pine hold October's
waning moon, the way the myriad
events contain the moment,
life diminishing as it grows.
Today we added chickens
to the flock, bits of reconstruction
for the coming months. Yesterday
the snow & rain & chalky light
marked a year completed in the hollow,
an abstract foreshadowing like a reptile's
handprint on an ancient beach.
Midpoint in our lives we cradle
firewood in arms, a prayer
in the heart. A goal
we carry into winter.

Blueline 5, no. 1 (1983)

Below the Clock

The light blue above your head,
the window wide below the clock
where we watched you leave tracks
all over the rolled flat donut dough,
fluffs of flour caught by the glass.
Punch the donuts you called it,
slapping one hand with its circular cutter
onto the sleepy white mass,
slap again, lifting out a circle,
circles that you lay in rows
on the long thin wire baking sheets.
These you lifted behind you,
descended into bubbling lard,
fifty pound blocks of white fat
now brown in the heat.
Bubbling your circular orbs high and brown
the fat spatted your arms.
You acted like mosquitoes had landed:
your hands full, you could not bat them off.
Later, your hands full,
full of me, my tender young body
quiet under your hands, your
hands curving now my shape,
rinsed of flour, dough, and sugar.

Blueline 19 (1998)

Fire Tender

I pray that God will send me fire tender,
One that will lie next to me
After tending the fire.

A fire tender stirs the coals
before he fits the seasoned wood,
Building a mosaic of blue, orange and yellow flame.

A fire tender is constant
He builds early
So you wake up to the muffled popping, snapping
of smoky sap cooking,

If a fire tender came to stay
I would leap with faith,
Unafraid,
And lower my feet
To the mystery of the floor.

Blueline 14 (1993)

ALLEN HOEY

Winter Light

The minister in the last scene of Ingmar Bergman's
Winter Light preaches to an empty church—
the organist and deacon alone, and the woman
he has, if anyone, loved, in the shell that rings
with music, then more with the stillness before words.

The camera renders a grainy black and white
world lacking the extremes. Trees darker
splotches against prevailing snow, the night
longer than any our latitude knows, yet
the grey pall is familiar, the drifting steam

and pockets of clarity. What word could he offer
to hold a man here, on bleak earth, lacking himself
strong motive to stay? God lingers,
if at all, in the wisps of smoke hard in the cold
sky, a distinct shape first from the chimney,

then yielding to cold in its oblique rise.
Where else would you find it? Love, too, hides
in the murkier greys, the dark rings at the bases
of trees where the trees' own heat keeps back the snow.
She is not pretty. She is flesh. A grey that fights

being grey. The one light thing that moves
warm in the night, the night that lingers
in the corners of day. What warms her?
In the end, the greys darken, thicken.
The few clear moments seem never to have been.

Blueline 9 (1988)

Rowing on the Sacandaga River

From one of the sun-glints on the highway overhead
I am a dab of paint on the scenery
Framed by some chrome window out on a Sunday drive.
Up there they do not breathe this sultry reek
Of steaming air and rotting leaves. They cannot see
The rise and dip of long white oars,
The pull and slackening
Of tendons beneath brown skin as I curl and flatten
back again;
Or how each stroke snags the water
Pulling threads of sun across its sheer green shimmer.

Oars folded in, I watch my hand
Dragging through the water,
Pale as the upturned belly of a perch,
Thrown back through pity,
Still gaping, still waving its shock-stiffened fins.
Once, they say, we stepped out from the water.
We cannot live there now.

Beside cement pilings, a heron shifts his legs,
Coils his neck back into his shoulders,
Blinking both pale eyes. Strange bird,
Feathered snake, given wings by mistake.
A bumped oar breaks his stance,
But through each flap of wings,
His neck holds proud,
Curved prow carved on pagan boats,
Arching above the ancient seas.

Mornings, rising from the depths of sleep,
That yellow eye again, that cruel beak
Will spear me through and lift me
Fighting to be thrown back into my suspension,

My stillness of green pools
Below the floating leaves,
Where dreams alight and flick their wings.

Blueline 3, no. 2 (1982)

Adirondack Winter

In Brooklyn
Where I grew up
Zero
Was mythic cold

Like in the old country
When I was a boy cold

Here in the north country
Cold
    just
Is.

It takes over
It sits in the trees
The sky
Is the color of cold

This morning
       it's only twenty below
In the February dawn
I take the garbage out at six A.M.
Rather than the night before—
So as to keep the varmints out of it

The snow crunches under my feet
     like corn flakes
The trees crack
Like rifle shots

The ice moans
On the lake
A mile away

Dressed warmly
I can't feel the cold

But I can hear it

Blueline 22 (2001)

Twenty-Five Naps in the Adirondacks

The nap on the slanting rock by the lake.
Odd that no bed is as comfortable as the right rock.

The nap of the young lovers
after they pitch their tent
in a private spot
back off the trail
and make love in the afternoon
on top of their rustling sleeping bags.

The nap of the two men who swim out to the island
and lie down on beds of pine needles in the sun
and doze to the breeze hissing through the pines.

The nap of those same two men
on the bank of the river,
the canoe tied to an exposed root.
They lie on the slope with their hats over their faces.
They are only fifty years old,
so they probably have another twenty years or so
to go on perfecting
this sleepy, delicious art.

The nap after supper on the lookout rock.
From below it appears to be suspended among the trees.
When you arrive there, it is a wide deck of stone,
still warm from the day's sun.
The pond is laid out below you, all its coves clear,
the hills roll away beyond,
and after gazing a while
you lie down and snooze,
attaining for once the elusive goal
of being simultaneously
solid and high.

The nap of the old woman in the big rocker
on the porch in the afternoon.

The nap leaning against a tree,
the heavy pack leaning against another,
waiting to be carried five miles more.

The nap you take while hunkering under your poncho in the rain,
hunched over in the position
which in gorillas we call "the rain posture."
They are the masters of sitting and waiting in the rain.
I think we learned it from them, in the forest of time.

The nap in the tent in the long rain that lets up, then deepens again.

The nap beside the pond where dragonflies abound.
They come and go.
Their feet are fine.
They are the delicate acupuncturists of sleep.

The nap wrecked by the horsefly,
and when you finally succeed in smashing him against your skin,
along comes his brother.

The nap back in the cabin after tramping all afternoon through wet April
snow.
You sit down beside the fireplace,
and rhythms of its large, rounded stones,
and conk out a while
in the company of a crackling fire.

The nap in the cabin
you wake up from hungry,
and eat a supper of bean soup, rye bread, cheese,
and a cold bottle of beer,
and you sit talking with your friend
and the simple fare is very good,
and outside the window snow is falling in the dusk.

The nap by the pond in late summer.
You lie down in the tall grass and disappear into it.

The nap of the solo hiker
who wakes up
and for several seconds has no idea where he is.

The nap you wake up from
to find that a deer
is gazing at you, quite close.
Among all the things that have been part of that silent consciousness—
nights wandering, the moon,
first light over the marsh—
now you are one.

The naps of the man and woman celebrating their 25th anniversary
by hiking to Avalanche Pass.
They doze leaning against rocks in the cool May sun.
They wake and have coffee, steaming from a silver thermos.
They toast each other with coffee.
Then they toast the huge slopes of glacier-scoured stone.

The nap on the sandy beach
on the big lake miles from nowhere
where no one else is.
The two of you sleeping up on the sand.
The canoe sleeping on the shore.

The nap in the lake,
not asleep but as good as,
leaning back, eyes closed, stroking now and then,
reclining in clear, loose hold of water.

The nap that has loon cries in it.

The nap by the creek descending through rocks
broken, rounded, balanced, and leaning
in a wild sculpture,

and in the moments before drifting off
you think about the sculptor.

And the nap by the waterfall.

And the nap by the waterfall.

And the nap by the waterfall.

And the great nap you have not yet taken.

Blueline 22 (2001)

Gothics

They sprouted from our roof at night,
last week of June. I was in bed
making mountains with my knees.
I backed across the street to Ciaranellos
and up a tall embankment where
their house should have been. Seven peaks
reared up like Matterhorns that I had
conjured in my sleep. I owned
the Gothics then—I must have been five
or ten. I studied maps and kept each profile
in my head. We used to come down
Blue Barns Road from Rexford and see them
poke above the Palmertown Range
but those were clouds—that lifted
and dissolved. When we had lost
our snow I liked to think they kept
it stored up there in caves.

And then I'd lie in bed and break
the flat world in a gray blanket.

Or last year: my sister wrote and said
they'd paddled a canoe up Indian Lake
past Sabael late September and watched those
snow peaks come up from my old dream.
Then the blanket would slip and my toes
get cold under the white sheet.

Blueline 13 (1992)

Map

My skin browns in April sun,
the map on my forearm emerges,
the old burn scar. (We were arguing,
remember? I spilled the coffee.)
Pale landmasses, blue rivers
that run to harbors, bays. If I hold
my hand out and face north, we read
how channel leads to channel past
islands, headlands, back to open sea.

But if we turn inland to the mountains
we must cross a long plain, hacking
trails through brush and hardwood
working upstream through beaver swamp
to high ground. Trees hide the pass,
we wrangle over which creek to follow
which slope to cross. The way narrows,
shadows are cold and smell of stone,
our thighs ache, mist closes in.
Then a stir of wind, ground falls away.
Breathing hard we stop and look back
into cloud. I lift the map. See,
we have come this far, let us press
deeper, moving towards a heartland
I am not sure we will recognize.

Blueline 8 (1987)

Above Sacandaga

On the bridge from Batchellerville
the teenagers flock,
doves on a wire
electric in their youth.
Thrill pilgrims,
they come to jump,
to leap frozen in the air
against green mountains,
to hang above Sacandaga
suspended over lakes of blue fire.

Rumors of concrete pilings
lurk in shadows
inches below the surface
of bright waters.
Just enough darkness
to justify their plunge.
Ten years younger
and I might join them in celebration,
in taking one more giant gulp of air
with the promise of so many more.

I drive by slowly; my speed
the limit of the bridge.
And seeing I'm not the Sheriff,
they drop like brookstones,
smooth and brown and slippery,
into waters drowning
with the souls of flooded towns.

Blueline 15 (1994)

The Orchard in Winter

Thursday:
Snow slants hard
across the silver
apple trees. Bolts
of blue, red, green
tumble and slide
down the hill
as if Fellini has brought
his circus to New England.

The sound of children's laughter
is like our own.

Friday:
And with morning—
another dazzling importance.
The old calligraphy of shadows
dark across the snow.
A sky more blue
than the last.
Apple trees shine
and stand so still
they are like dancers
bowed and waiting
for the dying
of our applause.

Saturday:
In another life
they were men of quiet importance.
Five crows sit
shining in the trees.

Sunday:

Except for the slow
hand of the sun
nothing moves all day.
Night falls.
I cannot take my eyes
from the pale moonlit boughs.

Monday:

I think I hear singing
in the trees this morning.
One ladder left standing
holds no one. The doors
to the barn still closed.
Not a single bird in the sky.

Tuesday:

At dawn
three deer come down
from the gray mountain
into the trees,
search for the chilled sweetness
beneath the melting snow.

Wednesday:

Try as I did all day
I could not conjure spring.
Nothing imagined is
as delicate as
the apple's blossom.

Blueline 22 (2001)

KATE O'CONNELL

Autumn Elms

Tenuous
against rose-glow sky,
they stand
every evening,
on top of the tallest hill
in Congress Park.

When I see them
they remind me
of tired women
who have forgotten
to pull down the shades
before undressing.

They have shed their garments
thereabout;
their summer ornaments
detritus now,
heaps
scattered on the ground.

I want to tell them
that they are beautiful,
still beautiful;
that their willowy limbs
are graceful,
graceful

as the arching arms
and tapered fingers
of Pavlova's dying swan.

Blueline 5, no. 1 (1983)

Cancelled Flights

Storm clouds
blow the gulls
across the field
billowing waves
of wings.

Wires sag
with the fluttering weight
of sparrows' feet
marching in place
on bare branches.

One crow caws
loudly,
raucously.

Geese cover the lawn
honking at the vanished sun.
The wind sighs into silence.
All motion stops
as the opened sky
pours out upon the
flightless feathers,
matting them
to the earth.

Blueline 19 (1998)

ALLEN C. FISCHER

Renoir's Fear

If snow is sickness
as Renoir feared,
then the clouds swarming
overhead are epidemic.
Once the storm begins,
there is no cure—bitter
words hit their target,
bury everything around.
Survival is not in question
but rather our understanding
of what is happening:
is it winter of the spirit
or just passing weather?
Although we're reminded
of firestorms and blizzards,
what transfigures this landscape
is neither hot nor cold,
sand nor snow but temper
out of control.

Blueline 22 (2001)

The Cat in the Diner

swerves under my table.

I am not surprised.
The prescription for my new glasses
is wrong: surfaces become
colors that move silently past
my feet, walls warp at a glance.

The villagers are calm. They talk
among themselves while
mountains tilt at their town.

I eat my lunch,
reach to pet the stray vision.

Blueline 21 (2000)

The Cottage on the Lake

Summer. Here are the hollyhocks,
pale yellow, pink, standing
as your grandmother's back. Here the lake,
flattened with lilies, full
with the tall milfoil in stalky clusters.
Every Saturday, a new week begins: a new family
trundles in the long dirt drive, the father
lifting duffels and coolers, the mother
unlocking the door, pulling open the shades.
All week, before anyone else rises, you're up,
alone, walking in your nightdress to the porch,
and beyond, to the lake's dark lip, listening
to the kingfisher's ratchet as he dives
from the cedar tree. The sky
lightens, and the day will feed
on everything you give it: the sawing voices
of your family, the mallards in their quiet steady swimming,
the secret you hold inside your tight thin chest
this summer on the lake, the summer you are ten.

Blueline 20 (1999)

Afternoon Sun, Zero Degrees

(Hayden Carruth's Writing Shack)

Zero. Sunlight.
River's gurgle
muffled under ice.
Where do brook trout go?
How does ice become them?
Their brains slow to tableau
vivant. To know ice that close-
ly! Then thrash alive in spring.

At Hayden's shack,
the brook's iced shut.
Only wordplay tugs
at my line, flashes
in the capped and hooded
head. Sparkle. Parka. Homespun puns in the ice of i-
solation. Whatever words

alone can do
they do. The heart's
another matter,
needing kindling, but
just now I'm out of luck.
My love life's frozen deep.
The old woodstove's no match for
this cold snap. My fingers freeze.

My hungers cease.
My arms encase
me, fused like wings. A
singing chickadee
flits tree to tree, bird-body

in league with cold *dee-dee*
of bird-mind. What does it know
of zero? It knows its body,

if not its mind,
will zip up limbs
looking for summer
bugs preserved like freeze-
dried peas. Jesus, where has
Hayden gone? How did he
outlast this cold, hold chaos,
snow, at bay. How? Why, love's

interventions:
warmth and wit, great
sense and sentiment
for dear Rose Marie,
dear *liebe,* who lives here
still, alone, still lively
in her age. She gave him his
voice, his cold peculiar

rage to chastise
others with love,
with *brothers, I loved
you all.* Bejesus,
he says now his mind is
moving toward zero, too.
Now his poems are frozen in
neural pools, each phrase encased

in musing ice,
unaware of
the silver sparkle,
flashing undersides,
one pool over—unless
sun in league with summer,

and love in league with matter,
melts the whole ice-dammed river!

Jesus, I'm heed-
less of zero's
estate. I'll study
how shadows—as sun
moves, heedless of us, crossing our afternoon—grow.
Imagine them—Hayden, Rose—
shadows lengthening by sun's

command, now swoon
across snow, lie
long in blue day's un-
doing, and marry
eventual sunset.
Fire's out. My fingers,
still numb, now cradle a match,
ignite the oldest news, try

to grasp what drew
me to this shack
from the start: his poems
that love spawned, imag-
ining I could unfreeze
the passions from the man.
I can't. He's blocked in ice or
swimming too far down to seize.

Blueline 22 (2000)

Impromptu Design

The still pond gives back
the cloudless sky   immaculate
the bird's beak plucks
an insect from the water-skin
sends the ripple circling
to the bank now the sky's
image is no longer seamless.
Corrugated.

Blueline 18 (1997)

Slight Change

We watch daily
from the bay windows of the farm house.
Finally the ice fingers
start to slip
off the crest of the hill
and curl down
into the palm of water at the base.
My 80-year-old mother says
she already thinks ahead
to summer flowers
wild and still
the way she's thought of them since childhood:
iris straining broken pen blue in the marsh
vetch, a hair tangle of purple
Queen Anne, white lace
like the doilies on her mother's dresser,
goldenrod spreading mustard on every slice of field.
She feels the stems
green in fingers.
Her knuckles knot with arthritis
only the gathering and holding are harder.
The flowers return perpetual, perennial like memories.

Blueline 18 (1997)

ELIZABETH BILLER-CHAPMAN

Summer Haiku, Fulton Street

I.

Now magnolias loft
their small vanilla clouds. My
daughter turns twenty

and the corn husk squeaks.
How greenly we fall: shelled peas,
July's deep round bowl.

II.

Fiery August
wilts the garden, my green wish-
bone. Again I fill

the watering can;
my tall sunflower pitcher.
Cold water, blue cups:

summer's concerto,
oboe d'amore. The moon
in Virgo—listens.

Blueline 17 (1996)

Georgia O'Keeffe

21: Texas

I do not know
what to call this state
of mind and body, beyond loneliness
and beyond desire, or what produces it,
but it wholly shapes my life:
the pressure of my blood
in its perpetual beating race,
the pressure of my thighs
as if clamped together
so as not to fly apart,
the pressure of the earth
in its bleeding curvature
and its long long arching ache
against the sky. I walk miles away
from town at night, and work
in charcoal on paper, black
and white, and forms take shape.
Something stunned and elemental
draws me to them.
Sometimes in watercolor
I permit myself blue.

35: Lake George

My eyes are reflected
in the irises of his.
I feel the brush
of my own fingertips
exploring my breast, my skin
the texture of an orchid,
and my body opened, white
beneath encroaching firs.
Clouds overhang the hills

and threads of mist vibrate on the lake.
I line my woolen shirts with silk.
In silver light
the barn glows fiery red.

81: New Mexico
Sunrise
defines the skull, the stones, the hills, the bones
in ochres and eggshell pinks and blues.
Everything alive is magnetized
by death and solitude,
the harsh poles of the desert magnitude.
When evening approaches
the sky gathers its space into its deep,
pressuring the horizon. Jack-in-the-pulpit,
purple and black. The sun sets
with the force of a thunderclap.
If I am to live in the present,
quickened and hot, showered with sparks
from the friction of telluric and celestial plates
ground against each other,
how am I to escape rapture?
In a single diagonal sweep
the umber line of a road
unifies earth with sky.

Blueline 5, no. 1 (1983)

Looking for Home

"Looking for home is like
looking for gold."
        —Attendant at gas
    station, Syracuse, 1968

We might be living in separate countries now.
In upstate New York, you peer from your window
on rainwater dripping from stiff green leaves.

The garden has never before been so abundant,
from asparagus to squash to strawberries to beans,
a harvest so precious you are afraid to leave it.
While the other night, quite late, I stood
at a fragrant pinon wood fire and alternately drank
of flames and starshowers over distant mountains.
In the polite tones of the tourist, I had asked,
"What mountains are those?" The answer came back,
offended surprise, "But Sangre de Cristos." Of course:
those that Georgia O'Keeffe had mined for blood
and gold. The faded peaks, drenched in the wash
of the star-flecked sky, seemed to float above
invisible seas. The prairies had been called an ocean
by the pioneers, and the Conestoga wagons
were prairie schooners running before the waves.
And O'Keeffe was born in Sun Prairie, Wisconsin.

She found a home in Abiquiu, arroyo wastes
and sage, absent trees. "I like some trees
between me and God," Nadine had said. For sure.
But here for miles and miles the sage brushes
over sand and clay spiked with marl. A waste
of possibilities, God's backhanded slap
at earth. Yet people try. Sitting with Henry
in his parched garden, I saw a green lizard
slithering by on stone. "For luck," he said,
and laughed. I laughed too, in disbelief.
I felt it cross my instep all that night.
I carry the East out here with me enclosed
in my heart, a little locked box concealing gold.
The West blows through the far mountain passes,
the breath of God exhaled, vast and cold.
O'Keeffe had walked for miles, for days, and found
in a mountain crevice, clinging, a nameless starflower.
Its petals shone like the leaves of aspens
quaking below. She painted petals and bones.
No one found this juxtaposition shocking—

a commonplace breed in the West—but I had stood
looking for long. The afternoon light was steeped
the color of tea or hay or mellow gold,
and would rise above the mountains, nugget-like, that night.

Blueline 4, no. 2 (1983)

Summer Wedding

Once, a generation ago, I was a bride in southern Italy.
In summer we lived near the coast in a two-room villa
Three centuries old. It was guarded by the gnarled, gray-green
Trees of an olive grove and abutted by a vineyard
Planted over Cuma, Apollo's ancient shrine,
The sibyl's grotto beneath, her lord's temple above.
In my day, the laurel still grew green
About the temple's broken steps and pillar drums.
Wildflowers bloomed between the paving stones.

Each afternoon I rested on those holy stones and read,
Or, somnolent with midday heat and pregnancy,
I'd scratch the forehead of a wandering cow, or look to sea.
Late afternoons, when I was cool and full of calm,
I'd wander back, and rising up from every step,
The sweet odor of wild thyme led me all the way home.
That was a generation ago, a hazy idyll lost
Before the memory of it was whole, the memory of thyme
I still call up, or laurel leaves beside a holy place.

Now you stand under a white and yellow tent
Beside an Adirondack pond in early May,
Dark water stretches out behind you.
Ancient mountains rise above, hallow you somehow.
You've wound forget-me-nots and everlasting in your hair.
You promise continued love, protracted peace,
Among the gray-green alders, the birches and your friends.
I've woven thyme among your wedding flowers;
May its warm sweet smell bless you on all the paths to home.

Blueline 4, no. 1 (1982)

Melancholy: Schroon Lake

It visits unannounced, uninvited
yet with bitter regularity,
a galling companion.

As I trudge through a summer spangled meadow
all wasted in buttercup and rue,
it steals from my purse of simple pleasures
and leaves a choking inertia.

But lakeside
it's a burlap dress flung off
so a bruised head,
buoyant with its new lightness
ascends to the sun
as clumsily as a trampled dandelion.

I slip into the water.
It tears like yards of silk
and the black sadness is no more
than silt below me.

Blueline 22 (2001)

The Algebra of a Solitary Wasp

It is an apple-blossom afternoon.
A wasp, fragile as anything that blooms,
purrs its way among the huge and hungry
until its arms are full of golden glue.

She's a whir of wings and honey dancing
in the wild wind. She knows when it means war.
The wasp can tell, before the yellow takes the lawn,
the time to fill her nest with taut victims

she has stung to stupor, piled like sticks
of bread, and tucked away like a secret.
She builds gray mansions of homespun paper,
jugs of mud, art as seen through insect eyes.

When she's done she'll lay a single white egg
on the warm chest of her choice victim
and seal up the nest for the long night.
A thing, ravenous, will emerge through time.

Caught between a prehistoric journey
and a destination of golden light,
a strange white worm begins its odd grazing.
By spring it will have chewed its mystery through.

Blueline 19 (1998)

Arrowheads

The ground along the creek is sharp
with points and flinty slivers, blades
of whetted quartz. After plowing
the sun picks out sparks of stone, tooth
and seed shaped, double edged. After
rain the soil is lit with tips of
arrows where all other signs
of culture have washed away, melted
into humus, the midden spoils,
bark hut, beaded sleeve. The worked stones
surface like a crop each year, make
the tilth abrasive, make the rows
a rough museum of human will
in flints that sailed against the flood,
of stones that flew and tasted blood.

Blueline 12 (1991)

Stacking Wood

I

am

busy with the bones of old trees,

stacking their neat lengths into columns,

three over three over three in crisscross fashion,

then piling them into the space between

with hollow, knocking sounds,

these tough wedges and thick loaves

cut to the length of a forearm or a thigh,

working them into a tight, sturdy rectangle,

exposed to the sun but firm against the elements,

hearing in them echoes of the wind they held,

ice rattling their branches, their devotion to the sun;

this is my architecture, my anchorage to the earth,

a stout pedestal for an airy, invisible bridge above,

sanctified by the kind of day this is:

when we are closer to nature,

the wind silvering the water,

cumulus clouds unfurling,

and the purposeful self

slugging log after log

into a resting place

until winter comes

and it is time

to release

their flames.

Blueline 21 (2000)

Taurus

Her bony back is pointed
and spare. I ride
surprised the way the bones
dig into my bones,
legs around the barrel
of her stony ribs.

Two thin cows scrounge
the rocks and weeds.
We three in the old orchard—
one to hold feet and boost,
one to steer the somnolent
beast, and I astride.

The boy who knows, goes behind
and cranks to make her start.
She sets off, a rough jog,
I bouncing, bone against bone,
for the closest apple tree,
barren and old, to scrape me off.

Under its long, bony arms
I fall on the rock-filled slope.
The hands that squeeze the milk,
tired from working on the road,
will find it sour, tonight.
But we don't care.

Blueline 6, no. 1 (1984)

Cement-Man

Cement-man weighs down the back
of his boat when he passes—
the motor groans and casts a huge
rooster-tail behind the gray-steel hauler.

Cement-man spends his holidays
lugging sand, gravel, and mix,
stirring, pouring, shoveling,
smoothing, and patty-patting.

Cement-man is building a cement patio
at the back of his cottage
because his charcoal grill tips
on the old Precambrian shield.

Cement-man built a cement dock
with solid steps leading to water
thus avoiding the mess of rocks
old logs, sphagnum moss, and laurel.

Cement-man likes his work concrete,
then he can feel it, and he knows it's his.

Blueline 6, no. 2 (1985)

LOIS MARIE HARROD

The Secondhand Sonnet

I am the small bird who, unable to make
her own silk, pinches it where she can find it:
the moth's shimmery bivouac, the orb spinner's
scaffold or, often in the meadow,

the cribellate's airy tease. I do not need
beauty, but stickiness and subtle strength,
a gossamer for speckled eggs,
a strand, a stitch, a purse of leaves.

Such is my beginning, the secondhand silk,
some say camouflage, coating her throat
in another's craft, but I have begun to say

ineluctable glimmer, for what I cannot
seam myself becomes light passing,
not through my nest, but through the trees.

Blueline 17 (1996)

Boarding 'Round

Stingy Mrs. Graham hides butter in the cupboard
Resents an extra mouth
Serves salt pork in slivers
Her dry eggless cornbread
Scratches my throat when I swallow

The Walshes have cats
Kittens curl about my ankles
While a calico scratches my satchel
At night I sleep covered in fur
Warm circles of feline contentment
The schoolmarm's nocturnal students

At the Taylors I am royalty
Little Annie offers me a blue ribbon
While Maggie begs to brush my hair
Ellen holds my chair and Lizzie serves my plate
Airy white biscuits
Smothered with steaming chicken gravy

I meet William at the Sullivans
Their chestnut colt is for sale
The handsome stranger checks teeth, feels legs
Gallops around the pasture
Next day, after school, he is there again
"Looking for a mare?"
Mr. Sullivan roars with laughter

Blueline 21 (2000)

Gill Brook

Gill Brook's clear water,
cold as drifting snow,
washes stone white,
carves in its passing,
hollows and pools
smooth and
graceful as snowdrifts.

Gill Brook's clear water,
never warm, never still, never silent,
teaches the pliant rock as it passes
that the world
is still forming.
Nothing is finished.

Blueline 22 (2001)

A Lesser Summit

A narrow path
sunk through grey-green moss
and lined with blueberry bushes
will lead you upwards
through wind-honed spruce
to the rounded rock
of a lesser summit.

Sit here and rest.
The forest stretches far
and farther yet the mountains' purple-blue
melts into blue-grey sky.
Watch where the hawks float languid
as a summer afternoon.

Sit and be blessed by sun
and scents,
and the silence
of a lesser summit.

Blueline 22 (2001)

Upstate, April

This spring loves me like blood, crazy
for my wrists and hands. It pulses
thin in its green misgivings. I admit
I'm surprised by its strict evocation
of water: mud, red bruises of swollen tissue,
xylem, phloem: the usual affair. But I'm ready
for winter to lift its beard off the
scraping ground. The whole sky
has done its penance. Listen: even the eighteen wheelers
seem grateful in their grinned gunnings past.
The highway distant, all loads are
a good-graced thrumming. Sound's
the survivor here. Through winter
it's been shutting us up with an absence, groaning
within the hardpan ground,
giving us all a bad rap for our bones,
hurting us with a hardness
of hearing, this soliloquy of loss.
We're better, now,
with our dingy faces clearing like a high-ground mark on the hills—
I can see them, as they've always been, painful, there
awkward as drunkards fumbling—
denuded, then wreathing, green-full
thrusting wet, sharped needles, all fir
writhing upwards towards the brim.

Blueline 15 (1994)

Evergreens

We ride the gondola at Gore alone
in April, and the mountains are not green,
but brown and beige because the chilly sun
has not leafed out the barren winter scene.
But here and there, in clump, and copse, and patch,
the evergreens spike up in vibrant sprays
and splash throughout the tangled forest thatch
their densely feathered tents of living cheer.
Their trick is to renew not all at once,
but stretched out over time, as though they knew
the harm of losing in a single bunch
the things that time and waiting patience grew.
       Much more than this high cable car, they lift
       our spirits up with their persistent gifts.

Blueline 22 (2001)

A Sacred Place

"Composed chiefly of metamorphic rock, the Adirondacks were formed as igneous rocks (mainly granite) intruded upward, doming the earth's surface; subsequent faulting of the earth's crust and surface erosion, particularly of the Pleistocene glaciers, have given the mountains a rugged topography, scenic gorges, waterfalls, and numerous lakes."

—*The New Columbia Encyclopedia*

Imagine some great hardened rocky dome
comes pushing like a mushroom through the earth,
as slow as time itself, in some huge birth
from softer folds of earth and sand and stone.
This helmet of a Titan dead and gone
a billion years ago reveals its worth
in dents and cuts across its giant girth,
protecting still old monstrous skin and bone.

We ride upon the rivers, lakes, and plains
that crumble slowly off the ancient crown
with wind and gravity and rinsing rains.
What rises up as we slide slowly down
unearths deep battle scars and ancient pains,
the enormous beauty of a sacred ground.

Blueline 22 (2001)

Three Haiku

Soft, silenced footsteps,
treading needles and wildgrass—
pine-scented forest

A chorus singing
on a late summer evening:
peepers by the pond

Ripples in water,
a flurry of commotion—
water-bugs dancing

Blueline 22 (2001)

In Braille

I am inhabited by a bird.
By day, it rests in soft turnings
as I move about the house,
talking to my children.
At night, when the leaves
are thick tongued and cannot speak
my skin thin as cellophane tears,
strings of tendon and sinew rip.
Nose and mouth harden to a beak
as breasts are feathered down
the bird claws through.
A red-tailed hawk circling
a sky unstenciled by stars
I am wind on stone.

Blueline 16 (1995)

Near Mount Robson, Canada

On the fifth day
I realize this meadow, this
outswelling of land between
icefields, this closewoven
solitary place,
is home.

There is kinship deeper than blood.
There is native land not defined by birth.

The marmots
who sit on their rocks to await the sun's rising,
who are the pan-pipes of this meadow,
whisper, long and lovely,
an invitation.

If it were summer forever
perhaps I would stay, nibble
spruce bark, swim in pools
pure enough to drink, follow
the mountain goats to their night-place,
enter with welcome a marmot dwelling,
go delightedly wild.

My feet are already buried
in lichen, heather, campion;
already accustomed
to wincing rock

As this meadow
fills me, I tear
a scar in its earth,
where a young marmot
may dig a new home.

The clear, fearless cries
of the sunrise watchers
drift to mountains
they only dimly see,
they have known all their lives.

Blueline 16 (1995)

Bloomfield Cemetery Est. 1860

She lies beneath wild peas
and browning grasses silent
these one hundred years a woman
who talked like knitting needles
drove her husband to the barn
in search of quiet. Well
he had bent too and was buried
beside her—opposite the children,

those who cried their sparrow calls
and were too soon buried: Emma 6 yrs.
Willie 8 mos. Henry 4 mos. Jas 1 yr. 6 mos.
and three tiny curved uprights reaching
eight inches toward the sky:
infant, infant, and E. C.

She must have lived each year
the same swelling, a doctor
galloping through the night,
delivery and too soon another
wrapped and boxed;
she but thirty-five.

Where did the live ones scatter?
There must have been some
who made it through winters, grew
old enough to move cattle,
fished those same high swells
that daunted Cabot two hundred years before.

None left to warm his tea, darn socks?
None buried in the family 'house'
laid out in concrete,
steps at the entrance.

Still the stones stand, some tilted
not yet vandalized by boys
with strong quick bodies who show
their mastery of death by shoving
weakened grave posts, whacking
infant slabs off at earth level.

This quiet family
halfway up the slope,
weather-sanded lambs of God
echoed by hillsides of Holsteins
cupped in tree-shaded hollows:
Willie the dove, James a lamb, Henry
a rose and Emma's clasped hands
above words now difficult to read:

> *I am dying! . . .*
> *Shake hands, and*
> *Kiss me good by.—*

Ocean winds keep the grasses nodding,
play the music of high trees.
Eucalyptus peels off
her pleated skirts. All the cypress
have fallen, their span done.
Still you endure.

Kiss me good by.

Blueline 16 (1995)

ELIZABETH WOODBURY

Ballet Lesson

Briansky
was the dancer of our town

With glowing ivory skin
black brooding hair
Shaped as frame to angular face
and dark infernal eyes

Laden with pale color
but deep in the hues of fragrance
were the lilacs of those afternoons
Lavender and lily white

Applauding the slow breeze of
Summer's full neighborhoods,
"Oh, the wildness of one stilled
Arabesque"

Blueline 14 (1993)

ROBERT SCHULER

skiing below zero: afternoon raga

wind sickles south   an afternoon's
sweat   hair   eyebrows   beard bristling icicles
sweater tightening bands of iron round ribs
thumbs   nose and toes numb
past the black scat of a wolf
squeezed out   bullets rifled into the icy
grooves of the salmon-pink ski trail
the barred owl who-who-hoots
wild high out of the blackest pines
racing the moon
skating silver over the river

Blueline 21 (2000)

Spring, March 21st

maple leaves spin down
silver in the wind
the hot black sprawl
of birds and branches and twigs
under this
cold clear bright blueness

Blueline 21 (2000)

6:55 P.M., June 23rd

light showers down
through the mountains
and canyons of grayblack clouds
streams silver-green
along the veins of the leaves

Blueline 21 (2000)

PAM FRENCH

Audubon Tapes

Driving white knuckled
From mountain green to smog city
I listen to Audubon tapes,
Everything familiar
I am leaving behind
And suddenly want to
Recognize, know:
The song of the wood thrush,
The red-eyed vireo,
The bittern's airy gulp.

Something familiar
To guide me by
Speeding cars
Cutting past me
Massive trucks
Blowing fumes.

And just when I hit
The Cross-Bronx Expressway,
The rich swell of an oriole's tune.

Blueline 21 (2000)

forget carl

forget fog creeping in
on little cat feet. Meet instead
the white vapor swallowing
my head, whole hog.

Wallowing, he devours
ships, the tallest redwoods.
Entire landscapes, coastlines
the size of Maine
drip from his soft gray lips.

Fed, he leers, gluttonous.
This pig can be butchered
but it takes an ax of sun to roast him.
Then he boils off, froth to the sky.

Blueline 21 (2000)

Cashew Cones

At the *Five & Ten* you could buy
A white paper cone brimming with hot cashews,
Wander out onto the cold street as I did
In Northern Vermont, my boot clad toes
Glacial as icicles and almost as pretty,
My nose an apartment house of good smells.

Sometimes the dead cold air would stall
Any aroma from wafting up,
Cashews becoming a ghost event,
The dry trails of smoky snow
Levitating just enough
To curtain the air in apprehension.

The snowman my friends and I made was no ghost on the hill:
His bright coal eyes, cashew eyebrows deliciously thick,
The halved carrot from which he breathed,
A punctuation and nearly perfect—
Perfection being what a child makes
From the empty hours stacked like wood against the house.

The plaid scarf our snowboy wore
Flagged across the wind,
While hourly, the melt-sun dripped him down
To the nearly nothing much—
A bright pool hollowed in the earth.

Today, there are no cashew cones.
So much gets eaten in order to stay alive.
When the steps grow slick as a skating rink,
And the front door jambs on ice,
Memory scoops me a coneful of cashews;

Delicious smells so strong
That I am always walking backwards into time
To warm my hands in a place I have been.

Blueline 20 (1999)

Pastoral

I've put a son
   on the ridge
      alone

         with rifle, shells, and binoculars;
      I've gone to Little River bank with bow and line
to hunt beneath the surface. There is an illusion
        between me and my target.

      "To hit the image
      is to miss the fish.

      You must aim at nothing."

        And since I can't
          get the hang
          of it,

            I'm wet
        from retrieving my arrow.

Sit on river bank to dry off. Watch this:
      skater bugs cut winds ripple; bass sulk past
        deep in their green haunt.
      Cedar waxwing sits in the sky. I see
          circles
      where fish die in fish mouth.

Clothes dry in sunlight; son's got me covered.

        A red fin approaches,
         so I reach
           for my bow.

Blueline 11 (1990)

First Flight, First Music

We did not ask for music
from this machine, as we accelerated
into that sequence of air filling
our valley. You tried turns,
level flight, leaned away from
gravity's yearning. Then the prelude
deepened; we followed pinon-studded
plateaus northeast to wild places.

Look! A herd of antelope, startled
westwards by our silver vector.
We bank sharply in a two-G arc;
the antelope, choreographed by
our own dance, veer back east.
Their colors change from brown to
white to brown again. Our shadow
settles swift blue upon the snow.
We race the course of the river
upstream, an ever-shallowing canyon
which widens into grassland.

Like clear notes from a harpsichord,
five elk are poised by the snowy
streambed, protected in the hollow
below the banks. Beyond a twist
of the wheel they are gone and
we hurtle toward the San Luis
Hills, a cluster of volcanic cones
modulating the plain. Sliding down
their south sides we descend to
the valley bottom. The sunlight
changes key to F minor and caught
in the beautifully inexorable beat
of a fugue we flee across miles

of snowy parabolas subtended by
sagebrush, carved by wind, cross-wind.
Our motion in that delicate space
between land and sky is a cadence
of voices of light and shape of man:
stone survey monuments, an old
railroad tank car, occasional
buildings humbled by the years.

I watch you sensing control pressures,
studying instruments: to you, it's
a marvel, fierce exhilaration. For me,
each flight is a new love, first music.

Earth reaches for our speed. We lift
over an area of timber and are
cradled by its convection currents.
On the horizon the slate blue line
of the Jemez is a long pedal point.
Comes the coda: the canyon of the
Rio Grande wheels underneath.
Suddenly we are home, slowed in
that sliver of air above earth,
turning left towards land.
The chirp of tire rubber on runway
reunites us with the ground,
whence so recent we rose
on the wings of the morning.

Blueline 3, no. 1 (1981)

Blue Mountain Lake

for my sister

At the edge of Blue Mountain Lake
the smell of pine unfurls like motel soap
we opened in some double-room of childhood.
I seem to see you bobbing still, a blue-striped cork
in a phantom, sun-scorched sea—blurring the tow rope
of the water skier, and his white wake,
and the boat which bends and disappears behind a wood.

I whirled, a scarecrow of a child
on my first amusement park ride, New Jersey,
both hands clutching the pin-striped wheel.
You leaned halfway across the world
to tell me, "pass the tea,"
so I did, sliding the make-believe pot to you, eyes wild
till you caught my hands and we both hung on for real.

One day we drove to Coney Island
and you went for a swim.
I let the ocean wet my feet, no more than that,
and kept a watchful eye on your phosphorescent bathing cap
till you re-emerged—except, it wasn't you, it was a slim
blonde shaking out her hair. I ran along the sand
crying, till I stumbled on you where you sat

staring dead ahead into the water,
dry as a bone.
You guessed the waves were too high, you said.
I only nodded, knees weak with relief,
but I dragged you home
as if you were my only daughter
returned for an evening from the dead.

Now I ask myself, the dutiful student:
How is this blue-capped mountain like you?
You, who are not monumental or stark,
why do you seem to sway at such a height?
You are like the color blue,
that's all. You do not represent
anything, you are simply what you are.

When the strongman's arms begin to break
from holding up the child, and the clock
winds down, I look
into the darkest corner of the nursery.
I find two girls still playing in the cracks
of light. Their silence makes
a sound like winter snowing in the lake.

Blueline 6, no. 1 (1984)

Speechless

Forward and back,
earth empties and fills
her bowl.
I gallop my feet in circles on the sand,
sun and wind wrinkling my face.
Nothing left to say.
Waves—speak for me . . .

Blueline 20 (1999)

ARTHUR McMASTER

Gathering Night Noises

They are, in the long ago summer darkness
over Fourth Lake, New York,

images on the precipice of dawn—
skittering again through my mind—
like Satyrs after Salome.

I am made to see, then, the corner
stucco store, now grown shabbily small,

where friends in their thin shirts
bought red-wax lips, paper masks,
and other simple treats.

It is, in the long ago summer darkness
where I lived as a boy,

my pale soul going ever so timidly
up the walls around me,
gathering night noises,

Putting them safely into the abyss.
Distant voices come to me

unbidden, blind in the shadow. I search
with every half-breath, growing faint now,
and finally still—by morning they are gone.

Blueline 22 (2001)

Meltwater

They don't know how it feels
when a sunwarmed key turns
in the ice's lock
and winter's heavy cell door
grudgingly opens
and cold's anaconda manacles
fall away.

They don't know how it feels
when you're loose,
when you flow again into springtime,
tumble in noisy somersaults
down mountainsides,
when you flex, expand, sparkle, overflow,
fill the ponds, the lakes, the valleys.

You want to run
up to everything
and kiss it,
embrace the maples,
lick the outcrop's granite nipples,
tickle the sombre leatherleaf
in its brown puritanical jerkin
until it giggles.
You want to inhale
the balsams' erotic perfume,
and peek into the darkness
under their skirts
while outraged blue jays shriek.

You hunger to whisper suggestive sonnets
to deadheads lolling half-awake
in the accelerating current,
and hug everything,

and spread the news
that things will be all right,
and bring new birth
to layers of gray leaves packed
flat as asphalt by the vanished snow.

They don't know how it feels
to be so misunderstood,
so maligned—
to be called "destructive"
while they build dikes and levees,
and count the days until I begin to shrink,
recede, become docile again,
tuck my flaccid manhood away
in the river's tight-buttoned bankers' pants.

For a while it's all right.
I go through my well-rehearsed routine,
tumble like a jaded circus acrobat
over concrete dams while tourists' cameras
click like ravens' busy beaks.

I, too, am torn apart:
my yearning for expansion,
for greatness,
for universal love
at war with these ordinary banks,
this well-worn channel,
this predictable route.
My own whitecaps mock me—
jeer that all my wild outpourings
can take me nowhere.

Yet the hunger never stops.
No choice but to keep flowing
here in this second confinement,
no choice but to trust

that this mapped-out river is
a route to someplace
big enough.

Blueline 20 (1999)

Prose

On Adirondack Porches

Nothing remains of the old white house in Warrensburg but a blackened wall
and part of its red and green porch railing. It had dominated the town's main
street for nearly a century, a full-skirted Victorian matron aloofly set back on its
acres of lawn. It had borne with dignity the fate of so many ample nineteenth
century residences in upstate New York, handed from owner to owner, to be
converted into boarding house, inn or restaurant. Then one night last March,
fire reduced it to a charred heap. It was still smouldering when we drove
through town the next day, and we were saddened by its loss. More than ever
we were aware of the fragility and transience of Adirondack history.

I was sad for other reasons. The house, with its turrets and gables and especially its encompassing veranda, reminded me of the old fieldstone house in
Colorado where I spent my girlhood. Many summers I spent on Willowcroft's
spacious screened front porch, built by my grandmother when we moved
there in 1948. It proved a perfect shelter from the hot Colorado sun and from
my industrious mother who was forever eager to put me to work. In the afternoons, however, she returned from her barn chores and the various demands
of some sixty-five animals domiciled on Willowcroft's ten acres, to join my
grandmother and me for an hour of sleepy conversation on the porch. Topics
were mainly current events among the animal populations; more serious discussions took place inside, in my grandmother's sitting room or in the kitchen.
When I succumbed to adolescent moodiness, I crept still further into the inte-
rior to the privacy of my bedroom. In the evenings my father emerged from the
house to settle himself in his great wicker armchair that commanded a corner
of the porch, and, feet propped on the companion footstool, soon fell asleep.
The porch was for summer and shade and dreaming; it smelled of grass and
cottonwood trees and, in those days, fresh Colorado air. It screened out mosquitoes and kept off the rain; neither inside nor outside, it was a place of transition, a threshold full of possibilities for a young girl sunk in a chair with an
open book and hope unfolding like a flower.

No wonder that I began to notice Adirondack porches when we moved
here eight years ago. On our way to and from Blue Mountain Lake, we usually
pass through Warrensburg, and there, until last spring, was the Victorian matron hemmed by her veranda and other houses scarcely less grand, sporting

fluted columns of the Greek and Roman style, soaring porticos in the best nineteenth century tradition, even double-deckers for second story residents. Outside of town dwellings become scattered and considerably more modest, but each has its version of a porch. Some are mere brims, umbrellas over a doorway; others, screened or glassed, are solid projections of the main building; still others, spanning several sides, are an open series of balustrades and posts supporting a slanted roof.

A few porches appear to have been built as necessary afterthoughts to shore up a sagging frame. Depending on style or whimsy, supports may range from chiseled colonnades festooned with webs of bric-a-brac, to crude logs propping up a snow-settled roof. However they are made, Adirondack porches have one thing in common—they are there for a purpose.

While I was enjoying my own porch at Willowcroft, I paid little attention to others, probably because they were merely ornamental or entirely absent on the new tract houses that characterized Colorado's post-war building boom. I did, however, make a vague distinction between the back porch and the front porch. On the back porch you put your old refrigerator, your trash cans, muddy galoshes and broom; on the front, your swing, your plants, your padded chair and yourself. You admitted your callers to the front porch, your dog to the back.

In the Adirondacks, there seems to be little difference between what is customarily relegated to the back and what goes on in front. Open porches afford the best view and often set me musing about the connection between the objects on display and the nature of the people within. Snowshoes, deer antlers, skis leaning against a wall, boots by the doorway, empty planters dangling from the ceiling, a dried wreath left over from Christmas—these are typical winter trappings. At one end is the mandatory woodpile carefully stacked—or an old refrigerator. In the fall, wool shirts and checkered hunting jackets droop from a row of pegs, a barrel of wild apples brims in the corner, sometimes a cake cools on a high shelf, out of reach of children and raccoons. Summer brings forth plants, chairs, and occupants who squarely face the road and eye the traffic drowsily. In all seasons, on nearly every porch large enough, laundry is hung at least once a week: snowy lines of underwear, blue jeans in five sizes, long red drawers, yellow and pink pastel sheets ballooned with wind or stiff as plate glass windows on a January day. A day's wash in winter is as colorful as roadside wildflowers in July, a welcome bouquet against the gray and white landscape. Many houses are equipped with automatic dryers, but their owners seem to prefer slow, rough drying in the fresh Adirondack air, rain or no, to fabric softener and static cling.

Adirondack porches today are decidedly less grand than they were a hundred years ago. Then they reached a peak of elegance only suggested by the ghosts in Warrensburg. The grand Adirondack hotels of the 1890s were noted for their verandas, or promenades as they were sometimes called. Here the city-born merchant and his family gathered to take tea, play games and stroll their afternoons away. The veranda not only allowed for social pastimes and perhaps a courtship or two, but also served as a border between the wilderness, perhaps all too apparent to some, and the familiar, civil world of the hotel. By the early twentieth century the great hotels and their summer promenades had disappeared, many of them burned to the ground. In the severe and frugal Adirondacks, their brief, opulent existence seems an anachronism, no more tangible than wood smoke.

The leisurely style of life represented by the old hotel veranda is as different from the life I led on Willowcroft's front porch in the 1950s as it is from what transpires on an Adirondack porch today. Yet all three share that sense of transition between outer and inner, a social pause or margin between public and private worlds. The porches in these mountains cautiously invite the stranger to enter by degrees into the intimacy of the home—but not before he has wiped his feet and discarded his boots. The porch is protector of the house, a zone of moderation allowing its owner to emerge by similar degrees from the warmth of his stove into the chilled and windy landscape. It is both a barrier to raw nature and a conditioner for those who have grown too soft within.

Combining practicality and sociability, the Adirondack porch, which functions as storage area, woodshed and laundry room, as well as a place to visit and enjoy the air, shows signs of surviving this century and perhaps the next. It is true that new houses without porches at all have invaded the region in the last twenty years—shaved, stripped, incomplete structures that look as if their hair was cut too short. These houses often undergo an evolution of sorts; they are encased with split, prefabricated logs or shingles and a porch is added. The other day I noticed a long, multi-posted overhang being attached to the side of a house trailer. A futile gesture to permanence perhaps. But to me, it was progress.

Blueline 2, no. 1 (1980)

The McDougall Girl

The news of the McDougall girl's death struck me to the core much more so than the deaths of distant and elderly relatives like Great Aunt Kate. We never knew each other, but that made no difference and in no way lessened the blow. She was vivid in my mind, slight and raven-haired. As my father drove us to the theater each summer evening, we often passed the McDougall girl trotting her chestnut horse along the dirt roads. I sat wedged between my older brother and sister in the back seat of our station wagon. Despite my siblings' pointy elbows digging into my sides, I would turn around and wave to the McDougall girl until she disappeared in our sweeping cloud of dust. She waved back, always.

I swore I had met her just nine months before her death. Whether or not this occurred, I cannot be certain. My recollection of the McDougall girl belongs with countless other memories of my youth which are veiled by a dense, unyielding mist. I no longer try to clear the mist. Much like a lie repeated time and time again until even the liar cannot differentiate between truth and fallacy, that memory has gained a tangible vividness.

It was in the Variety Store, Labor Day weekend, our last days in Minerva before heading home for another school year. We were buying clean notebooks and unsharpened pencils, and our spirits were weighed down with back-to-school melancholy. For the first time the McDougall girl and I both had our feet planted firmly on the ground, she horseless and I unpinned from the back seat of our car. Though I was younger, I towered far above her. She held me spellbound. I was unable to take my eyes from her face as she bought a pack of Juicy Fruit gum. She held me captive, the angel of my nighttime prayer. "Angel of God, my guardian dear, to whom God's love commits me here, ever this night be at my side, to light and guard, to rule and guide." Watching her in that dimly lit store was like stumbling upon a wild rabbit or a deer in our back fields. A deep awe, an overwhelming wonder overtook me, just as if I had been crouching in our pasture, so still, peering at an unsuspecting rabbit as it burrowed into the earth. Fear came next, a dread of moving even slightly with a sudden blink or a swallow that would cause the timid animal to start. I believed the McDougall girl was unsuspecting of my steady eyes, since she did not seem bothered; otherwise I would not have been so bold. Then she slipped

150 ⮐ THE *BLUELINE* ANTHOLOGY

a stick of gum from its yellow paper and held the glittering aluminum towards me with her fine hand. "Here you go," she spoke and smiled, just a bit, before turning to leave.

Only nine months have passed since that day, seeming like both an eternity and a flash, and now a group of men arrives dressed in black and orange hunting jackets. They are preparing to dredge the lake for the McDougall girl. There is no air of sobriety about them, there are no somber faces. They tell jokes and smack each other on the back. I wonder if any of these men knew her. They could not possibly be her father, her brothers, or her uncles. One man, clad only in a black T-shirt and blue jeans, assumes leadership. He flexes his arm muscles while using his hand as a cleaver to slice the lake into sections. They divvy up the sectioned territory. "Pff," I give a wave of my hand. "They'll never find her here," I say just as the noon whistle blows. The men drop human-sized hooks into the lake, breaking the water's still surface. I shiver.

"We've got to search for the McDougall girl," I say to my cousin, Renee, as we sit watching on our horses. "No Minerva search squad's gonna find her. They don't even have their own policemen or firemen. Just plain old volunteers. Know what that means?" Renee shakes her head without interest. "If there's ever a fire, nobody's in the firehouse. They're all sleeping in their own houses, so that means they have to get dressed, drive all the way to the firehouse," my hands clutch an imaginary steering wheel," and then finally, they get into the fire engines and go to the fire." I abandon the steering wheel for a firehose and aim it at the group of men. "By the time they got to your house there'd be nothing but cinders." Renee cocks her head in a so-what manner. "That's why we've got to start a search team. These farmers don't have time. Know that whistle we just heard? There's one at noon and one at six so the farmers know it's time to come in and eat, or else they'd just stay out forever and starve. We have to find her. Don't you want to be a hero? Maybe they'd put our pictures up in the post office."

Renee says nothing for a minute. She's wearing the same stony face she's had on for days, a look of determination not to give into the sadness she's been feeling. Renee twists the reins of her bridle around her fingers until they turn blue. "Only criminals' pictures get put up in the post office."

I shake my head and stare off at the aluminum canoes along the shore. The water is murky-gray, reflecting sunless sky. "She's not dead," I mutter.

"That psycho already confessed. Only thing he didn't say is where he dumped the body."

"He's lying," I snap.

"Look," Renee responds, "I'm here to forget my problems, forget about my Dad."

"This'll take your mind off things. You like riding. We'll ride and search at the same time."

"Nah," Renee reaches down and rubs her horse's head.

"Come on. We'll wear these magic goggles to help us see better," I say, pulling out the swimming goggles from by backpack.

"I don't want to find any dead body."

"I told you already, she is not dead. Don't be such a chicken. Chicken. Buck, bu-bu-bu-buck!" I flap my arms.

Renee hisses, "Grow up."

I toss her a pair of goggles and we trot our horses back home. We are silent. Acres and acres of young corn are visible through the trees of the wooded road. I spy through my magic goggles to try and discover the McDougall girl in the thick brush. Perhaps she's bound and gagged to some tree. There is so much land to cover, even in a small town like Minerva, and already I am discouraged. The vegetation will grow quickly in the weeks ahead. I used to pray for the corn to shoot up overnight so we could play hide-and-seek in the tall concealing stalks, and gnaw on sweet, buttered cobs at supper, but now my father's once cherished words sour. "The corn grows so fast you can see it shoot up right under your nose."

It is cool. We are clad only in swimsuits, matching tanks of soft blue cotton my mother gave us a few days before. School has been out an entire week. It's the beginning of our summer vacation, and our sudden freedom makes us indifferent to the chilly temperature as well as the saddle sores between our legs from riding pantless. My eyes are drawn to Renee's black hair which flies into the air in long waves, then rests briefly on her white back before becoming airborne again. "Angel of God, my guardian dear," I whisper, remembering the McDougall girl's black tresses as she rode along on her horse. I am determined to find her. She is not gone.

Nearly home, at the top of our steep road, we reach Mr. Stone's cottage-sized house. He tips back and forth in his rocker, its cane seat sagging from his weight. His sole companion, a twenty-year old tabby, is dozing on his lap, lulled by the ocean-like movement. The front door of his house is open as it always is during the warmer months, except when he makes his weekly trip to town for his groceries or to the local cemetery to visit his wife's grave. Through the screen door the sounds of Mr. Stone's television and radio blast, both on full volume.

"His nephew's the one who confessed," I inform Renee as we ride by and ignore Mr. Stone's waving hand. "That makes him a suspect too. Guilt by assassination. We'll have to search his house as a last resort."

"No way!" Renee shakes her head angrily, her large green eyes twitch uncontrollably. "What's your problem? How can you talk so loud about his nephew just as we're in front of his house?"

I snort, "He's deaf. Didn't you hear how loud his t.v. and radio were on?"

"How do you know; you've probably never spoken to him?"

"Course I have," I glare at my cousin. When we reach the stables I say, "You look a little like her, you know."

"Like who?"

"The McDougall girl."

"So what."

I slap my thigh. "I have a great idea! We'll use you as bait. Maybe Mr. Stone and his nephew are like the Son of Sam. They go after the same kind of girl. We could kill two birds with one stone. Catch them and find the McDougall girl."

Renee's eyes are glistening as her twitch intensifies. She aims her goggles at me like a slingshot and lets them fly. "If you don't quit this, I'm going home for the summer!"

"Good job," I holler, dismount, and pick up the goggles that landed in the grass. "You broke 'em!"

"I'm going home." Renee rides off.

"Your mother doesn't want you at home!" I scream after her.

After storming around the barn trying to decide how I can find the McDougall girl alone, I begin feeling hungry for lunch. A long wail startles me as I approach our house. I stand motionless. The sobbing builds. In a faltering voice I ask, "Who is it?" But I am certain she is bound to a tree somewhere on our property. As I near the crying, I spot the raven-haired girl in the largest of the apple trees. He tied her to the upper branches where no one would have spotted her. "Mom!" I tear away screaming. "Help us!" I reach the window of my mother's study where she is busy at the typewriter. "Come quick," I plead through the screen.

Until my mother emerges, I lean against the cool brick of our house and try to compose myself. I entwine my arm securely around hers before steering us toward the apple tree. "What is it?" my mother asks. Her brow is furrowed. She walks briskly to the base of the tree. My heart ices over. "Sweetheart?" The McDougall girl's crying stops and all is quiet.

"I want to go home," she cries from above.

"What's going on here?" my mother demands of me.

"Sarah says my mother doesn't want me."

My eyes fall to the ground, burning with shame and the embarrassment of my mistake. My mother waits for me to look into her steel grey eyes and explain myself. "I didn't mean it," is all I manage. Not only haven't I found the McDougall girl, but I also got myself into unnecessary trouble.

"You owe your cousin an apology," my mother insists.

"Sorry," I offer.

"Now come down, Renee, and we'll make some lunch," my mother smiles up at her hopefully.

"No. My mother wants to get rid of me just like my father."

"Nonsense! She wrote you a letter today telling how much she misses you. We thought you girls would enjoy spending the summer together. For heaven's sake, come down and be careful. You can call her tonight and see how wrong you are."

Renee shimmies down backwards. Her back still heaves from the aftermath of her cry, like an infant who's badly shaken after a fall. She lands with a soft thud.

My mother sighs, relieved to have her niece back on the ground. "Give your cousin a hug," my mother lays a heavy hand on my shoulder and steers me towards Renee. I hug her half-heartedly and we head inside for lunch.

After my mother's returned to her study, I pull Renee outside and hiss under my breath, "Just because you have problems with your parents doesn't mean you have to try and cause problems for me." Renee doesn't say a word in her own defense. She stares at me with a vacantness in her cool eyes, then turns and walks away.

The first week of my search is drawing to an unsuccessful close. The Minerva searchers have had no success either. I pray every night with a devotion I've never known before. One evening, I am certain, we will see her on the roads of Minerva, riding her horse as we make our way to the theater. There was once a girl who was buried alive by her kidnappers. They made a special coffin for her with a light and an air vent, and she was able to survive. Still, my hope is beginning to fade.

Renee and I are still not speaking, except to keep up a front for my parents. She packed up her belongings from my bedroom. I had emptied half my bureau drawers just for her, cramming my clothes into wrinkled balls. She closed my trundle bed and moved to the guest room. It was just as well. At six every morning I wake up to search the cornfields before the farmers start up their tractors. Renee likes to sleep undisturbed.

Our dog, Lotte, is my one faithful companion. Each morning she comes along. We tear down the rows of corn, Lotte sniffing the ground with her keen nose. Sometimes she gets distracted by a crow or another farmer's dog, but she always returns. On the seventh day of our search, Lotte and I are in the fields by sunrise. I feel like an explorer as we squeeze through the rows of corn. The long leaves wrap themselves around my bare arms and legs, and the damp soil soothes my bare fee as they sink into the earth. This is the last field we will search. My feet plod on, my arms move rhythmically, held straight out to separate the leaves of corn.

When the noon whistle blows I am shocked at how quickly the morning flew, but then it seems as if it has always been noon and as if the whistle has always been blowing. It's the same odd feeling when you return to a special place not visited in a long time. A feeling that you never left, that a part of you remained there and now it is the other places that are nonexistent and foreign. To me there is no other world but the world of the cornfield. And each night when I close my eyes, I see myself slithering down the rows, I feel my hands pushing the coarse plants aside, and I sense the urgency of finding the McDougall girl as I begin to doze. The last field is now almost complete. Just two rows more. Mr. Thomas is nearby on his tractor. I duck down making sure my head is not visible, and I command Lotte to stay. At the end of the two rows we still have found nothing.

After dinner that night I excuse myself and go outside. My cat shoots out from our garden of tiger lilies and spins circles about my feet while the barn swallows swoop down at her. They are defending their nests. As I sit and lean my back against the peeling red barn, the back door of the house slams, and I see Renee is looking for me. She glances about with one hand shielding her eyes from the sinking sun, then spots me and shuffles towards the barn. The barn swallows shriek. Emily darts under my legs for cover.

"Your father can't keep up with the tomatoes. He wants help picking tomorrow."

"Wasn't my idea to plant tomatoes."

"You eat 'em, you should help."

"I eat them because I'm forced to," I retort. "Besides, I'm busy tomorrow planning the search of Mr. Stone's house."

Renee stares at me in disbelief. "No way. What is it with you? You didn't even know her."

"I sort of knew her," I mumble.

Renee sits down beside me. "When people die it's horrible," she says softly. "In some ways it's worse when they just disappear." She looks towards the hills. "I mean, I know my father's alive, but he just disappeared, he just didn't want to be with us anymore. One day, out of the blue, he must have stopped loving me."

"He never writes? Never calls?" I ask.

"Nope. Nothing."

I get up, not knowing what to say. Emily follows. Halfway to the house I glance back at my cousin who is still leaning against the barn. She is tapping the ground with a long stick like a blind person trying to get her bearings. She looks so forlorn in front of the massive barn. "Come on in," I call out, "before it gets pitch dark." We stroll towards our well-lit house, my cousin and I.

The next night, as soon as darkness has fallen, I pad down the hallway of our house and descend the stairs to the front door. Renee is crouching by the banister upstairs. She peers at me through the railings like a caged-in animal. I shoo her away and place an index finger to my pursed lips, "Shhh!"

Climbing the hill to Mr. Stone's house, I stay in the brush along the road-side. My ankles become raw from the wild raspberry bushes. Soon his house is in view, and I forget the scratches, concentrating instead on the light burning from his two downstairs windows, like a pair of evil eyes glaring in the darkness.

At last I reach his property where I lean against a weeping willow tree until my breath is caught. The thick hanging branches conceal me. The night is extremely cool, but I am flushed and slightly feverish. He sits on his front porch. He waits patiently for some passerby to stop and chat. Rings of smoke float from his cigar up to the porch's ceiling, and to the floor he drops the dark ashes, taking care not to get any on his cat.

Like a sleepwalker I approach Mr. Stone's back door, and not until I am standing in his dimly lit kitchen do I awaken with my chest heaving and my palms clenched. All is still. On the counter is an open box of Twinkies. The box has been torn apart as if a hungry raccoon had come across it. Above the kitchen sink is a calendar with a monthly photo that shocks me, a curvy blond clad in a pink bikini which vanishes when I lift the plastic film up and down, wondering why such an old man would have a thing like this hanging in his house. Mr. Stone's cupboards are disappointedly bare, leading me to believe that he might be packed up to flee town at a moment's notice. The cellar door is directly off the kitchen, but I decide to skip it for the time being and move on to the living room.

The old man can be seen through the screen door, rocking to and fro. He is talking to himself, convincing me even more of his insanity. "I like a good ride myself," he says outshouting the television, "but I'm getting too old." I bend over and peer under his sunken couch and then behind his lazyboy chair which is relaxed in its fully-prone position as if an apparition rests in its seat. When I open the hallway closet I find the most incriminating evidence yet, a gun rack holding three different types of rifles. I run my fingers over the smooth wood and cold metal parts, never having touched a gun before, and I wonder if those shots I've heard on still summer days have come from Mr. Stone's rifles and at what he's been firing.

He is talking to himself again as I reach the top of the stairs, skipping every other step to lessen the chance of hitting a noisy board. "You don't say!" he cackles. His bedroom is dark. I shine my flashlight in search of a lamp and find one by his bedside. After switching on the light, my hands settle on an old photograph of Mr. Stone and his wife, taken when they were newly married. She is propped upon a high chair like a princess, clothed in rich fabrics, her neck encircled by lace, her hands covered by white gloves and held in a prayer. Mr. Stone is so young and handsome. He stands proud, gazing at his wife with devotion.

As I flick back the bedspread my heart gives a jump, expecting to find the McDougall girl dead under the bed, her mouth distorted by a freakish grin of death. But there are only the dust-covered floorboards and a few dirty tissues crushed into tight balls. I eye the closet as my heart makes its every beat known, and after tugging open the door find only a few items of clothing. Then a weak chirp startles me. It comes from a shoebox on top of Mr. Stone's bureau. I shine my flashlight into the box where a baby starling, with its beak open wide, is pleading to be fed. The box is packed with hay in imitation of a bird's nest. Next to the box is an eye dropper and a shot glass filled with mushed food. I fill the dropper and squirt the liquid into the bird's beak. Baby starlings. We've had many fall down our chimney. My mother taught me to raise the baby birds until they grow feathers and have the strength to fly away. We keep them in a safe place, away from our curious cats, and when my mother feels it's time for the starling to be set free, we go out to our back field on a bright day and hold the bird in the palm of our hand until it feels courageous enough to flap its wings for the branches of the nearest tree. One summer our baby starling returned long after we had set it free. Suddenly, as my mother was doing her morning weeding, it soared from the sky and perched on her shoulder. Mr. Stone had not seemed the type to save a baby bird.

As I head back downstairs, Mr. Stone is still talking with a mouthful of Twinkie thickening his voice. His tabby licks up the crumbs. I escape through the kitchen and run for cover beneath the weeping willow where I can have a clear view of the old man through the wispy branches. Mr. Stone is not alone, however. It hasn't been himself he's been talking to, but my cousin who sits calmly on her horse's back while she eats her own Twinkie.

"Good, eh?" he asked Renee.

"Ummm. I love Twinkies even better than Devil Dogs," she agrees unnaturally loud.

"Like 'em both myself."

I wave frantically at Renee, hissing soft "psst" sounds. When I finally capture her attention she screams, "Gotta go now. It's getting late."

"Bye now," he says. "Don't be a stranger. Next time bring your little cousin along, and remember ya don't have to talk so loud, I ain't that deaf," he chuckles and then coughs on some Twinkie crumbs.

I run down the hill until I'm certain Mr. Stone can no longer catch sight of me, and there I wait anxiously for Renee.

"I was there the whole time you were inside, keeping him from walking in on you."

"I didn't need your help."

Renee nervously twirls a strand of her horse's mane. "They found her," she says in a low voice.

I begin to feel dizzy. "Who? They found the McDougall girl?" Renee nods. My voice does not seem like my own. It sounds far away. "Where?"

"Some farmer's field."

"Can't be," I say, crouching to the ground.

"It's over now, Sarah."

"You're a liar. Tell me what he did it for!" I scream.

Renee holds her hand out to me. "Get on," she says.

"Tell me why!" I demand.

"People don't always have reasons for the bad things they do."

Renee's hand is still held out. It is trembling and warm as she helps me up, or maybe it is me trembling. I don't have the spirit to argue anymore, so Renee rides us slowly home as I cling to her with my remaining strength.

That night I sleep in the guest room with my cousin. I have a dream. The McDougall girl and I are riding our horses down the wooded road to the lake. She is just a little ahead of me, gliding on her chestnut mare, almost never touching the earth. Though I try to catch up to her, leaning into every stride, I cannot close the distance between us. It isn't until we reach the lake that the McDougall girl finally slows, and turns, but then I see she is no longer the Mc-Dougall girl. My cousin, Renee, with her long black hair falling down around her pale face, waits for me to reach her side.

Blueline 15 (1994)

Jed's Grandfather

Jed slowly worked the handle of the back yard pitcher pump. He watched the water lap from side to side in waves as he tilted the bucket back and forth. The patterns of the dream were still going through his head. They hadn't been rinsed away with the first splash of water from the trough, water so cold that a paper-thin layer of ice still had to be brushed away these early spring mornings. Washing his face usually cleared away whatever cobwebs of sleep still clung to his face and his thoughts, but it hadn't happened this morning. The dream was still with him.

The swallows had flown up now. The red sun was a finger's width above the hill. He looked up and watched the swallows darting, diving, stitching the face of the sky the way his mother's needle covered a piece of cloth. The other birds, shorter winged, fluttered in groups, as if afraid to fly by themselves the way the swallows did. The swallows were the adventurous ones. He remembered how his grandfather had first pointed out to him the way a swallow can dart down to the surface of a lake and scoop up a mouthful of water without landing. They had watched swallows doing that, drinking from the pond below the house that day last blueberry season when Grandfather had rowed him out to The Island.

Usually the sight of the swallows in the morning sky would drive everything else out of his thoughts. He'd arch his back, lift his chin, hold out his arms a little. "Be a swallow, Jeddy," his grandfather had said to him. "Feel the wind under you? Lean a little to the right, that's it. Now, take her slow, you're coming down. Now, open your eyes. You're back to human again."

That wouldn't work this morning. The dream was with him. He was in the boat, dark water widening between them. The old man stood there on The Island, unaware of the great dark wave coming at him from behind. He was unaware because his eyes were on Jed and Jed no longer had a voice. He couldn't call out, he couldn't move his arms. He wanted to turn into a swallow, to fly back and rescue him, but he was paralyzed. Then the water between them began to open like a crack in the earth, like the earthquake he had heard his Uncle Randolph Dunham talk about having seen in far-off California.

"Jed!" It was his mother's voice. Jed looked up, noticing for the first time that the bucket had filled and was overflowing around his feet. A chicken which had come up to peck hopefully at his feet was scurrying around the edge of the spreading pool, now and then lifting up a foot and shaking it as the water touched it. Jed carried the bucket into the kitchen. His parents were at table. He hefted the bucket up onto the sink shelf.

"Getting stronger every day," his father said, his thin hand around a steaming mug. Behind him the wood stove crackled, making a sound Jed had always loved. The smoke from his father's coffee rose through the cold morning air of the kitchen. Jed could smell the coffee. It was a hearty smell, just as good but not quite the same as the smell when he ground the beans in the coffee mill with its blue enamel sides. But the dream was still with him. It was coming between him and the things which were ordinary and good and pleasant in his life the way a thick fog comes between a boat and the land. He was on that boat. He didn't know which way was home. He didn't know which way the tide was taking him through a fog ten times as thick and grey as the smoke rising from his father's coffee.

Jed's mother smiled at him, wiping her hands on her apron. *I know that,* Jed said to himself. It was the first time he had really noticed the way his mother always wiped her hands on her apron before she spoke when they were at table. She used the same care with her words that she used in making their food. All around Jed were familiar things, things he knew and loved, but he was seeing them for the first time . . . the small crystal dog in the east window where a bull's-eye pane of glass concentrated the sun like a prism and painted a rainbow on the wall near the stairs . . . the woodbox with its splintery top which always caught his left thumb when he went for an armful of kindling . . . the rocking chair that was empty now, the chair that always caught the last rays of the setting sun. . . .

"He takes after his . . ." his mother was saying. She stopped in mid-sentence. Jed knew why. He finished the sentence in his own mind. *He takes after his grandfather.* Jed's father was a good man, a hard-working man, but he had never had the strength of his wife's people, the Sabaels. That was why he worked clerking it at the store in town three miles from the farm. It was Jed's grandfather, straight as an ash, who had always done the work around the farm. Jed was only ten, but he was enough like the old man for people to notice.

"Jed," his mother said, her hands pressed against her apron, "you aren't eating."

The pancakes were dry in his mouth. He knew they were good. They were the pancakes his mother was famous for at church socials. They were light and smelled of the goodness of a summer wheat field, but he couldn't taste them.

Instead he tasted the salt air of the open boat, felt throbbing against his temples the pressure of the storm building around him, the storm that was lifting that great dark wave.

Jed's father was saying something to his mother. What was it? Jed hadn't heard him for the roaring of that storm.

"Are you sure?" his mother said.

"You're his daughter," Jed's father answered. He answered in the same quiet voice Jed had heard him use when he answered a customer who had asked what he should buy to get rid of the potato bugs or whether the percale was what she really wanted for her money's worth.

Jed's mother rose and walked over to the stove. She took the plate which had been warming there and covered it with a cloth. She put the cloth-covered plate and some silverware and a stoppered bottle into a basket. Jed recognized the basket. It was one his grandfather had made. He remembered the sound of the mallet as his grandfather pounded the side of the felled ash to break loose the strips he would trim to size and weave. His grandfather had shown him all of the steps many times, shown him by doing. He felt as if the way of making a basket had been woven into him the way the pattern of a web is woven into a spider's limbs. The old man's father had taught him that craft, a craft passed down for more generations than the Sabaels could count, passed down long before Jed's father's people had stepped from their ships onto these shores. For a moment the thought of his grandfather's sure hands weaving a basket drove away the dream. Then the pounding of the mallet became the pounding of waves against the side of the boat and he saw the old man's figure dwarfed by that lifting wave.

"Take this down to the Little House, Jed," his mother said. She was holding the basket out to him. Jed looked in her eyes for a moment and then reached out his hand for the basket.

No smoke was rising from the chimney. If it had been rising it would have traced a perfect line across the face of the bay and The Island. That was the way smoke rose on spring mornings such as this from the Little House his grandfather had built down where the field fell away, green becoming the grey of stone, the red of rockweed, the blue of sea. At the end of the little wharf a small boat was tied. It moved with the water, moved the way a horse will move when tied to a rail . . . not pulling hard enough to break free, hardly even putting a strain on its tether, but showing in its motion how anxious it is to be on its way. The boat was still there. But there was no smoke.

Jed drew in a breath, feeling a stiffness, a catch in his throat. But before he could call out he heard his grandfather's voice.

"Come," the old man called, making that simple word one of more meanings than one. It meant that he knew who was there. It meant that Jed was welcome. It was like the words in the old language his grandfather hardly ever spoke, the language Jed knew he still knew. It meant something else, too. Jed pulled gently at the locust post which held up the small open gate. It creaked as he pulled at it, but the old wood was still firm and supple. A locust post can stay in the ground for a hundred years and still bend any nail you're fool enough to try to drive into it. A hundred years. His grandfather was seventy-six years old.

Jed went in. John Sabael was sitting on the edge of his cot. There was a blanket around his shoulders, but his feet were bare. There was no rug on the floor and no fire in the stove. There hadn't been one for the last five days. It was cold in the Little House, but not as cold as Jed had thought it would be. There was a faint scent in the air, one which Jed had never noticed before. It confused him.

"That's how it smells, Jeddy," his grandfather said. "Don't pay it no mind."

Jed looked at his grandfather. John Sabael had always been a tall man, but never one whose frame had put on bulk. His shoulders had been broad, but not heavy, his arms long and sinewy unlike those of the others in town whose work took them out to pull the nets or up-river to cut the trees, not that ham-thick sort of arm which turned to softness and fat with age. Like an ash tree's limbs, that was how his grandfather's arms were. But now, after five days, there was a different look to his grandfather. There was a hollowness in his face that made the bones stand out. His eyes, fallen back into their sockets, seemed to be hiding in a shadow which had wrapped itself around the old man like the blanket about his shoulders. As he sat there, his hands grasping the edge of the bed, it seemed as if his shoulders were folding in around his chest.

Jed held out the basket. "Mama sent you this," he said.

"I'm glad she let you come," his grandfather said. He didn't reach out his hands for the basket.

"I wasn't sure I wanted to before," Jed said. "But I understand now." He heard his own voice as if it were the voice of a stranger. Yet the words the stranger spoke were ones he instantly recognized as the truth.

His grandfather nodded. Very slowly he got up from the bed. It took a great effort. It seemed to Jed as if he were watching something happen which was strange and wonderful, as magical as an ash tree uprooting itself and stepping across the woodlot. John Sabael walked very slowly to the back door of the Little House and opened it. Jed followed him. They stepped out into the light from the bay, a light which made Jed squint his eyes from the brightness. His grandfather sat down very slowly in the rough wooden chair, the one which faced The Island. Again Jed smelled that strange sweetness, but now he knew what it was he smelled. It was his grandfather's death.

Gulls were swooping above and in front of them now. They were grey and white and from their yellow beaks came those raucous squawks which had always seemed, to Jed, to be the one thing that linked them to the rocks they had flown up from. Those voices, rough and filled with the earth, were all that kept the gulls from flying up and up forever until they blended with the sky.

John Sabael made a small motion with his hand and Jed took the top off the basket. He removed the cloth from the plate. The heat rose up to touch the back of his hand. With his fingers he broke the pancakes up into small pieces. Then, piece by piece, he tossed them into the air. Swooping, diving, squabbling in mid-air, the gulls caught them all. Not one piece touched the ground.

Blueline 1, no. 2 (1980)

Flea Market

Crosley approached the edge of the highway, stopping to check for traffic before he tugged the loaded wagon onto the asphalt surface. The going was easier there, and he was just short of the crown in the road when Milton jerked past him.

Smart ass, Crosley thought.

His words were good voodoo, for no sooner had Milton hurried by than a lampshade toppled from his over-full box, spun twice on its rim, and wobbled to a stop just west of the center-line.

It was a better break than Crosley could have hoped for. He hiked it towards the far side, shoes hitting soft gravel just as a car swept out of the long turn to the north. He paused there to count the seconds until it passed, tires squealing and horn blasting angrily as Milton huffed to safety.

"Living dangerously," Crosley warned.

Milton continued on to the table without a word. "The chairs are wet," he said. He pulled his into the sun to dry.

Crosley continued to ease his wagon down the embankment stopping at the bottom to rest before he attempted the slight, grassy incline. He managed the three long steps, and arrived at the table. "I don't care if mine is damp," he said, "I'm sitting." He sat, stretching his tired legs in front of him as Milton arranged his half of the table.

When Milton was finished, he said, "I'll unload the wagon for you."

"The hell you will," Crosley answered. "That's *my* wagon."

Milton shrugged: his usual palms-in-the-air, infuriating shrug. "All right," he said, "I'll go to the barn."

Crosley was about to ask "what for?" when he saw that Milton was already halfway across the road. "Go on!" he said, and in his anger, he pushed himself up from his chair to get to work. Even standing was an effort at his age. His vertebrae, like the fish mold and the egg beater, were rusty. Of the dozen or so other worthless sundries he had collected, only two were of real value: a conch shell from Florida, and a piece of fluorite he had found in the quarry behind his niece's home in New Hampshire. He held it in his hands now, a chunk of sea-green crystal as big as his fist.

"Look at this," a voice said.

Crosley glanced up to find Milton standing above him. The morning sunlight burned and fuzzed at the boundaries of his familiar-looking body—narrow through the shoulders, wide and soft in the ass. But there was something else, too, slung across his hips like a saber.

"What in hell is that?"

"A sword. I found it in the barn."

"I thought you found everything there was already?"

"Not this," he said. "It was buried in bat shit. Completely buried."

Crosley felt the old resentment well up again. As if he, at his age, could go gallivanting around in barns, climbing ladders that were nothing but slats nailed up a wall. The lucky scavenger! He had found a butter churn first, then a sled. The churn brought fifty dollars, the sled forty more.

Remembering that, Crosley eyed the saber with pecuniary eye: the sort of piece that would have swung from a general's belt, on horseback.

"What's the blade like?" he asked.

"Got me," Milton said. "It's froze up."

Crosley smiled, feeling the old upper hand return. "Frozen, my ass. You can't pull it."

But Milton wasn't trapped so easily. "Here," he said, "try it yourself." He offered the saber to Crosley: three feet of metal sheath, tarnished black.

"The hell," Crosley said. He lifted a paperweight and blew the dust from its glass dome. He polished it with the heel of his hand and set it back in place, waiting for a customer.

They both waited; but none came.

"How much do you want for that pen-knife?" Crosley said at last. Milton smiled, folding his hands proudly around one knee. "Fifty dollars."

"You'll never get it. Not unless you find someone man enough to pull it."

Milton didn't answer that. The sun went behind a passing cloud and came out again, brighter and hotter than before. A car passed, and ten minutes later, another car, but neither driver slowed or even turned his head.

Milton got up and changed the position of his pieces.

"We need a sign," he said.

He had been saying that for two weeks, and for two weeks Crosley had given him the same answer.

"If they want it bad enough, they'll stop."

But Milton wasn't listening. He sat down and stood up again. "They don't see us," he said.

Crosley decided to ignore that remark. "Where's the can?" he said.

Milton reached into his box and pulled out the empty tin can they used for their kitty.

"Now put some money in it," Crosley said.

No answer. There was no need to repeat what Crosley had already explained: that an empty cup tends to stay that way. He rummaged in his pants pocket, found a crumpled dollar bill and flipped it into the can.

That kitty had been intended for beer money, originally. But after the sale of the churn and the sled, Milton had begun to think of bigger things. He got the idea of taking the bus to the city for a ball game. Three hours over in a diesel-smelling bus; three hours back. Four hours in between, sweltering under a hot sun. That was fun?

No, if it had been his money alone, Crosley would have taken the bus north to his niece's home in New Hampshire—*without* Milton. There, he'd spend an old man's vacation: sleeping late, watching the birds. Afternoons, he'd stroll to the neighboring farm and discuss the weather and the latest crop of heifers with the old German grandfather. And in the evening, when his niece was home, they'd share a leisurely supper on the porch and recall a family that was, for the most part, dead: Uncle Horace and Aunt Katherine, Grandfather Minkler, and the rest.

Another car passed without stopping. Almost on its tail came a big Cadillac. Crosley felt his heart quicken—city *money*—but as the car drew closer, he saw that it was rusted out and driven by a black man.

Milton stood up again. "I'm going to make a sign."

Crosley started to say "what for?" but Milton had reached the edge of the highway before he had a chance, looking doggedly left and right, and legging it to the far side.

He should know better, Crosley thought, trying to act so young. But you could get away with that at sixty-four. In a few years, age would catch up. His arteries would start to shrink or a knee would seize. Then he would know.

A trailer truck passed by, kicking up a storm of dust. Truck drivers stopped down the road at Rua's for coffee and eggs. They didn't buy antiques. Neither did the redhead who drove by in a beat-up Plymouth, a raccoon tail flapping from her radio antenna.

Nothing came by after that; not even a breeze. Just heat, rising from the road in curly waves that distorted the trees on the far side. Crosley sucked a horehound for his throat and wondered what sort of ridiculous sign Milton would come up with: SALE TODAY, with balloons tied to it? CLEARANCE?

Then he heard a car, coming down from the north as most of the others had.

As soon as he saw the old-fashioned grille and headlights, he knew it was a Mercedes. He watched the driver turn his sun-glassed face towards the table. The car, almost imperceptibly at first, began to move over towards the shoulder. The tires rolled quietly to a stop in the gravel, and the side window hummed down.

"Charlie, how much for the sword there?"

"That sword?" Crosley said, lifting himself high enough to see it. "You won't find many like that."

"How much?"

Crosley looked at the car door, as sleek as polished stone, and the bright white neck of the man's polo shirt. He thought about the fifty-dollar price Milton had set, and then he doubled it. "One hundred dollars," he said.

The black door opened—no creaks, nothing but the well-oiled click of machined parts—and the driver hopped out. He wore white shorts to match his shirt, white socks, and tennis shoes. His skin was very brown, as if he were of Spanish descent.

He sauntered over to the other end of the table and lifted the sword from the spot where Milton had propped it. He hefted its weight in both hands, then wrapped his right hand around the hilt and tried to draw the blade. He was gentle at first, but as the blade resisted, he increased the pressure of his pull. The muscles in his short arms bulged—but the sword was locked. He released his grip, paused, breathed hard two or three times, and tried again. This time the tendons in his neck stood out like wires, and his mouth contorted into a grimace. But the effect was the same. The blade had not budged even a fraction of an inch.

Crosley relaxed in his chair, allowing a smile to flicker across his lips.

"I've seen them like this before," the man said. He reached into his hip pocket while he was speaking, removing a roll of bills held together by a silver clip. He slipped two out and laid them across Crosley's open palm: fifties, both of them.

"Got any more where this one came from?" he said.

"I don't know," Crosley said. "Have to look."

"At least I got one of them," the man shrugged. "Let the next guy make some money, right? This'll bring a thousand in the city."

That figure barely registered in Crosley's mind; nor was he offended by the amount of profit the stranger might make. He was focused on the money in his hand, so completely that he never saw the Mercedes leave; nor did he notice it was gone until the fine orange dust of its departure had settled over the table.

His mind was made up by then. With a quick look towards the highway, he leaned forward and slipped one curled fifty into the can. The second he folded neatly in half and dropped into his shirt pocket. Then he sat down.

There was no sign yet of Milton. No doubt he was still in the barn, muddling around in his workshop. No one had a messier workshop than Milton, an amateur's shop if there had ever been one, littered with dried-out paint brushes and dulled tools. No wonder his work was bad.

Crosley settled deeper into his chair. The air had grown hotter, rolling in from the highway in slow, almost nauseating waves. He thought of a turtle on a hot day, and how they get caught sometimes crossing a road. There were turtles in New Hampshire. They walked up out of the stream below his niece's home, dusty black shells decorated with black markings. Nothing bothered a turtle. They couldn't do much if it did: couldn't run, couldn't bite unless they were on top of you. But they were old—hell, *ancient*—creatures. How had they survived all these years?

He was thinking of that when he saw Milton emerge from the shade-blackened barn door, carrying a sheet of plywood that covered all but his head, hands, and feet. He was almost to the edge of the road when Crosley saw that a message had been sprayed across the surface of the wood. Somewhere near the center line, the fuzzy windings collapsed into words: FLEA MARKET.

"They can't read that!" he hollered.

But Milton had already taken a sharp left in the gravel shoulder. He headed north at a brisk clip for about fifty yards before he stopped to prop the sign against a convenient boulder.

Even at the age of sixty-four, he looked beat as he hoofed it back in the heat. "That ought to do it," he said, rubbing his hands together.

"Maybe," Crosley said.

Milton took his same spot behind the table. A couple minutes passed before suddenly, and with a fair amount of agitation showing in his voice, he said, "*Hey!* Where's the sword?"

Crosley lifted his head slowly. "What sword?"

"The sword that was lying against this table!"

Crosley paused, pursing his lips and tapping them with the tip of an index finger. "Oh, the sword," he said. "*That* sword. I sold it."

Milton half stood with the shock. "You *sold* it? For God's sake, what did you get for it?"

Before Crosley could answer, Milton reached for the can, banging its contents out onto the table. The crumpled dollar bill—Crosley's seed money—

tumbled out easily. But the new fifty, curled tightly to the inside of the can, did not follow.

"Where is it?" Milton said.

Crosley eyed him curiously. He had never seen him quite so angry, the false good humor burned away for a change.

"The *money*, God damn it!"

Crosley paused. "Look in the can."

"What do you mean, in the can? The can is empty!"

Crosley smiled. He tilted his head back and folded his hands on the table like a schoolmaster. "Give me the can," he said calmly. "Give it."

Milton hesitated, then obliged. Crosley licked the tip of his forefinger and, with great ceremony, reached into the mouth of the can. His hand stirred inside momentarily, and then he drew the missing fifty into the light, stretching it end to end like a freshly washed sheet.

Milton leaped with joy. "Sweet Jesus!" he exclaimed. "We can go to Boston!"

"Not I," Crosley said.

But Milton was too exhilarated to listen. His face flushed with triumph. "Fifty bucks! For an old sword!"

"Old sword?" Crosley said. "That was some piece of steel."

Milton came up short. "You saw it? He pulled it?"

"Of course he pulled it. He was a young man. Powerful."

"And how was the steel?"

"The steel was beautiful. You know what he claimed it would bring, in the city? A thousand dollars."

Milton sobered a little. "Ah, they all say that," he said. "Who's gonna pay—"

But Crosley was no longer listening. His attention had been drawn to a blue Olds, swinging over from the northbound lane. Its muffler throbbed as it eased onto the gravel shoulder and over, edging so close to their table that the car door, when it opened, came to rest with a slight shudder against the table's metal rim.

The driver was no more than twenty, a fat-chested kid with blonde hair curling up out of his T-shirt and a big cigar poised in his right hand. "You the guys sold that sword?" he said.

"Sorry," Milton said. "We sold out of that."

"*I* don't want no sword," the boy said. He held the cigar up and surveyed it, from the damp, chewed end to the ember smoking at the far tip. Then he slipped it back into his mouth. "I want the money."

Neither Crosley nor Milton moved. The fat boy's eyes shifted from one to the other, and then his round face split into a grin.

"Maybe you didn't hear me," he said.

There was a slight movement behind the car's partially opened door. Crosley saw the small, black hole of a handgun peek out over the lip of the window. "Put that down," he said.

The boy gave a silly, almost embarrassed laugh—as if some girl had shown him up. "You can't tell me nothing," he said.

Milton leaned closer. "Give him the money," he hissed.

Crosley held the fifty in his hand. He looked at the boy again.

Then he stretched his arm forward and slipped the rolled edge of the bill between the boy's fat fingers, their little nails chewed deep into the flesh.

"Now where's the rest?" the boy said.

"What rest?" Milton said. "That's it."

The boy laughed nervously again. "Don't bullshit me. I talked to a guy down the road said he paid you a hundred dollars for a sword. Now it's your turn."

A brief silence followed. The boy turned his head, looking up the road and down it. He pushed the gun closer: "I *want* it."

The silence persisted. It was bad for all of them, but worst for Crosley, whose fear was compounded by the knowledge that Milton would soon find him out, discovering that he had lowered himself to the level of a common cheat. And for what? Pocket money? Pride?

He might have confessed everything—but he had no experience in confession, no practiced way of laying the soul bare.

Then the car came, approaching from the north at a speed faster than usual.

The boy heard it first. His head jerked, and a look of childish panic registered on his face, before his gun-laden hand leapt to the edge of the table and went off.

For what seemed like a long time afterwards, the world hung in stunned silence. It was like the moment before death, everything that had been, always, now reduced to three: an impenetrably blinding light; the smell of gunpowder; and, from somewhere a long ways off, the solitary tinkling of a bell. Following that, came a darkness like death.

But when Crosley came to, he was not dead, he was lying in the roadside grass while a familiar voice above him chanted, "He's gone! He's gone!" so unmistakably that he recollected everything—right down to the fifty dollars still tucked into the right breast pocket of his shirt. He sought the money now, holding it aloft, turning the folded bill in his fingers as he smiled not into the light of Our Lord, but the befuddled eyes of his housemate Milton.

"It's *yours!*" Crosley said, "the money! It's *yours!*"

Blueline 9 (1988)

Sabattis Falls

Sabattis Falls was situated just on the edge of the woods, just past the band of
sandy soil that was once the verge of a great northern sea, where the rivers that
now ran northwest through what had once been the bottom of that sea and
then turned northeast and ran into the St. Lawrence, had themselves once de-
bouched into that sea and deposited there the mud and gravel and sand that
they had worn and carried from the mountains that were once high and rocky
and now were rounded, old. The Sabattis was one of those rivers and the town
had straddled it where it pierced the rim of that plateau, that boundary, almost
dammed by it but falling through a narrow gorge. The river had been the carrier of the logs down off the mountains and the source of the power with which
they were sawn into lumber and thus the source and carrier of the town itself at
the first place on it where there was breathing room enough for a town and soil
enough to feed it and its horses. Or just almost enough for almost but not quite
a town, never incorporated or official, and never sure if it were permanent or
not.

It straddled another kind of boundary too, located as it was just past the
last marginally feasible agricultural land as you went south from the St.
Lawrence valley with the land generally dishing upwards toward the northern
foothills of the mountains. The settlers had not known that, or had not needed
to. They had cleared and built and farmed it anyway since the land below to
the north was already taken fifty years before they came; or perhaps because
they weren't really farmers at heart anyway and just wanted to be higher up
and closer to the hills and deer and trout; or because they came for the logging,
and only farmed to raise hay for the horses that were used in the woods in the
winter. Winter was the heart of their year, the logging season, the brush and
hardwoods leafless then, the swamps all frozen, the woods roads iced and
smooth; not the hot and muddy, black-fly and mosquito-ridden summer. So it
straddled that other kind of boundary too, almost as sharp as if it were drawn
on a map, between the more or less civilized and stable communities of the
lower northern part of Olmstead County and the not long ago wild and road-
less and almost trackless forest of the southern part; between the safe and
peaceful and tame and orderly, and (in the mind at least, in the imagination)

the lawless and dangerous, the fierce and careless and respectless, the half-forgotten but persistent wilderness.

It was never intentionally founded and settled at all, like the towns below in the valley, by merchants and farmers and millers that came seeking more space and deeper soil from New Hampshire and Vermont and Massachusetts, and brought their temperance and stores and schools and churches with them. The men that came to log the woods to the west and south and southeast along the rivers and tributaries big enough to float logs in the spring runoff were young and rough and mostly single, and a lot of them were French Canadians and a lot of the rest were Indians. They outnumbered the first women perhaps twenty to one, so that if they thought of marrying they probably couldn't and if they did marry they didn't think of themselves as settling because as soon as the logs in any given purchase were gone the company went broke or moved away, and they would move or go broke too. So it was only a place of transients in a transient industry to begin with.

That was the way the town had been right up to 1925 when even the shore of the magnificent spring-fed lake seven miles away in the woods, the northernmost good-sized natural lake in the mountains, had been stripped bare of the last accessible virgin timber in the county, and the pair of drunkards that had timbered it had gone bankrupt in their turn and left a million board feet of logs to sink to the bottom, and the land around the lake went over to a trust company way over in Watertown, that could never get it off its hands until after the Depression and halfway through the Second World War. Even much earlier than that, in the eighties and nineties, the accessible and marketable timber within reach of the mills at Sabattis Falls was all gone and the Bryant family that had built the Rapids as a hotel to serve the rich from the cities in the southern part of the state had started up a chair factory, just to keep the town alive at all, keep its schools and churches going because they at least thought it was, because to them at least it was, a town. And then the logging railroads came, the roads went further in the woods, the market grew for hemlock bark and pulp, and the town kept on, primitive, not conscious of itself historically, but just repeating and regenerate like the seasons, wintertime by wintertime.

There was competition between men, in strength and skill and courage in those days, between Frenchman and Frenchman and Frenchman and Indian; for skill and speed and strength with the double-bitted axe in the winter, and balance and agility and courage on the river drives. Men rode to their deaths on the logs, like the almost mythical Jean St. Jean Baptiste, for nothing but courage, or for competition in it—a profane and detailed historical man like any other no doubt but unremembered now as anything but demigod and ladies' man and one courageous fool, who rode the logs singing, and picked his day, and died when he was ready, and floated up among the logs above the dam one day and gave the place his name.

Blueline 6 (1984)

The Four Signs

"Decay is inherent in all material things."
        —the Buddha

I

Old Age

The night Paul stayed over with his grandfather, they spent the evening watching westerns and sit-coms. His grandfather never laughed. Just sat on the beat-up sofa and half-smiled at everything, occasionally mumbling in Polish. There were no lights on, and the TV lit up the living room in an eerie, blue-white glow.

When the news came on, his grandfather said that it was bedtime. The old man moved slowly up the stairs, his hand tightening on the rail with each step. Paul walked up behind him, impatient at the slow pace, but keeping back just the same.

When Paul got out of the bathroom, his grandfather was already in bed. Paul got on his pajamas and knelt at the side of the bed to pray. The old man said nothing, lying very still. After the prayers, Paul turned off the light and groped his way to the side of the bed. It was an old bed, with rope supports instead of wooden slats, and Paul felt it give as he crawled in. Getting under the covers, he felt the heat of his grandfather's body, which smelled of hay and sweat. The boy lay on his back, almost rigid.

"Good-night, Paul," the old man said suddenly out of the darkness.

"Good-night, *Djadgi*."

Paul closed his eyes and listened to his grandfather's breathing grow slower, softer. The boy sighed. He missed his own bed. The room had a strange smell, a combination of dust and dried manure. The farmhouse creaked in the wind of the late spring night. There was a thunk over his head, as if something had dropped a piece of wood in the attic. Paul's eyes snapped open. Moonlight filled the room now, and he looked at the bedroom in the cold white light. There was an antique chest of drawers, topped by a large mirror. A coat rack stood in the corner, covered with work shirts and overalls. A print hung on the far wall. Paul could not see its details in the moonlight, but he knew it was a listing of all the Polish kings, with dates of rulership and palm-sized color sketches, all faded to dull browns and reds.

The old man snorted in his sleep. Paul turned to look. The moonlight lit up his grandfather's hair, like a shimmering halo. His face, covered in the day's stubble, was starkly lined and worn.

After a time, Paul stopped peering at his grandfather and settled back, closing his eyes. He looked forward to the morning when he'd have the whole day to play on the farm. He tried to picture his favorite spots, the hayloft, the pine woods, the stream through the pasture, but all he could see, in the dark, was an afterimage of his grandfather's old face. The face grew larger as Paul grew quiet, until it loomed over him like a full moon in winter, dominating his slow slide into sleep.

II

Sickness

One hot summer's evening Paul's father took him to the circus. It was a small circus, with one large canvas tent spattered with dull-green patches, and several side-show wagons.

After the main show of clowns, fiery magic acts, and acrobats, Paul and his father were ready to go home. But as they left the main tent, the night air cooled their sweaty faces. They began to wander through the side shows. They all cost extra, but not enough for the father to begrudge the treat. The freak show boasted preserved two-headed dogs and a three-armed baby. Another wagon contained terrariums with tongue-licking lizards and seven-foot black snakes.

The last wagon held the big cat cages. It cost a dollar fifty. The father paused, his broad face frowning. He brushed his white, crew-cut hair, and then asked Paul if he wanted to go in.

Paul heard one of the cats growl. "Yeah, sure," he said.

"O.K. Here's the money. I'm going to stand outside and wait."

Paul paid the doorkeeper, a burly man wearing a greasy brown vest, and went in. The place reeked of dung. Under the dim yellow bulbs stood two rows of five cages, with knots of people staring in. No one smiled, and everyone was quiet except for the cats, who pounded their cages with their pacing.

Paul started down the aisle between the cages, looking quickly at the tigers and mountain lions. The cages were small, with just enough room for the cats to walk a couple of steps and then turn. They watched Paul, their open mouths dripping saliva, never ending their meaningless march.

About halfway down Paul stopped in front of the Bengal tiger cage. He was lying down, and panting heavily, his chest and sides pumping like a beached fish. Mucus covered his half-open eyes. Paul gazed at him for a moment, transfixed, and then walked out of the wagon, not even glancing at the other cats.

Outside Paul's father gave the boy a hard stare.

"You weren't in there very long."

"There wasn't much to see."

"You should learn to take your time and study the animals. Don't just rush through."

Paul didn't know what to say. He just wished he hadn't gone in.

"Are you ready to go home?" the father asked.

Paul nodded. His father took his hand and they walked back to the car, leaving the circus's strings of bright lights for the hot night's darkness.

On the way home, Paul's father concentrated on the unlit rural road. He turned on a country-western station and asked Paul how he liked the circus. Paul answered that it was great, and with the miles, the memory of the Bengal tiger faded, buried under bright clowns and flashy magicians.

III

Death

When Paul was old enough to handle a shovel, he started helping his father transplant trees. Paul's father, to supplement his income at the factory, had planted his ten acres with blue spruce and sold them after work. A big customer was the town cemetery. In the spring and fall, the best times to transplant because the tree's growth was dormant, Paul spent almost every weekend helping his father in the cemetery. They would dig a two-foot hole, and place the young, waist-high spruce in it. Then they would fill in the roots and gently tamp around the tree, firming the ground. The final step was to pour two buckets of water on the new soil.

The needles pricked Paul's skin, and at the end of the day, besides sore muscles, he'd have welts on his wrists and arms. And yet Paul liked the work. He enjoyed the smell of evergreens and being out in the sun and air.

The first fall Paul worked he witnessed a burial. He'd been to his grandfather's funeral, but this was different. This was the part the bereaved don't see.

He and his father paused while the gravediggers worked. First they lowered the casket. There was a drawn-out, ratcheting sound, then a loud sickening thud. After taking down the grave's canvas canopy, they rolled in the backhoe, heaving in buckets of dirt. Finally they smoothed and packed the grave with shovels and tossed the flowers on top. Through all of this, the dark-suited undertaker sat on a stone, calmly smoking his pipe.

After it was over, Paul and his father went back to planting trees. Paul noticed that his father kept watching him, peering up at his face between shoveling dirt. They got two more trees in. There were five left.

"What do you say we call it a day?" Paul's father asked.

Paul stopped tamping the tree they were finishing, confused. His father always planted the trees they dug up.

"We can water the burlap around the rest, and get them in tomorrow. They'll last. I think we've done enough for today."

Paul glanced back at the grave. The men were packing their tools in a rusty green pick-up truck. The backhoe was already rumbling down the dirt road, and was nearly out of the cemetery.

"All right," Paul answered.

IV

Asceticism

It was a cold winter's night, and Paul was glad he was in his friend's van. The engine was running with the heat on, so the van was warm, almost stuffy. Paul had his coat off. Outside, the light from the gibbous moon blended with the blue electric glare of the street lamps. There were mounds of snow by the street, but the pavement and the sidewalk were clear. They sparkled from ice crystals scattered over their surface. The night was bright, vibrant.

Inside the van was dark. Actually, the entire van, inside and out, was painted a dull black. Paul sat back in the darkness, smoking a joint. It was Friday night, and he and his friend, Greg, were getting high, listening to the FM rock station, and staring at the moon and ice.

The streets were deserted. Paul watched the bridge, past which the street took a turn. Every so often, as a car pulled onto the bridge, the light from its headlamps burst into the van. When this happened, whoever had the joint lowered it below the dash until the car passed.

After the fifth car, a figure dressed in a black overcoat, pants, and hat came down the street. He was the first person the two had seen on the sidewalk.

"Look," Greg said. "It's Father Dauwen."

Paul peered carefully in the moonlight and made out the white rectangle of the priest's collar.

"Sure is," he said, sliding back in the seat as deeply as he could go. Father Dauwen was a tall, slender man, with a pale, angular face and white hair. He was a good friend of Paul's father and had buried Paul's grandfather.

"What's he doin' out?" Greg asked.

"He goes out for a walk every night."

Paul watched the tall, silent figure stride silently down the sidewalk. As he drew close to the van, Paul could make out his face, and the white, ghost-like clouds formed by his breath. His face was calm, certain.

Paul ducked his head into the shadow of the van roof, away from the window. Finally, Father Dauwen walked past the van. His pace never slowed, and he never turned his head.

Paul and Greg sat for a moment and finished their joint. The radio burst into a string of commercials. Paul felt restless, disturbed.

"Let's head up to that party at Pete's," Greg suggested, sweeping back long, slightly greasy brown hair.

"I'm not up for it," Paul answered quietly.

"Should be a good time."

"Maybe."

"Come on, Paul. Let's do it."

The debate continued as "L.A. Woman" by the Doors replaced the commercials. By the song's finish Paul ended the discussion.

"I'm not into it. You can drop me off on the way up."

"Fine."

Greg threw the van in gear. He K-turned on the street, took a left on the state road, and headed north at sixty. The village's last houses soon fell behind, and the highway wound through farms and woodlots. The van was becoming too hot now. The engine whined and rattled. Greg turned up the radio and a raucous heavy metal hit rammed its way out of the cheap speaker.

Paul anxiously looked for his road. When it came he turned to Greg.

"You can let me out here."

"All right."

Greg slammed the van into lower gear and began furiously pumping the brakes. The van came to a violent halt.

"Thanks."

"Sure."

"Have a good time at Pete's."

"I will. See you tomorrow maybe."

"Right."

Paul got out and slammed the door. The van roared off, its blue exhaust visible in the moonlight. Then all was silent. Paul began to walk home, feeling good to be out in the open, in the icy pure air. He breathed deeply, clearing his lungs and his head. His mind sharpened, the pot high dissipating into the night. The stars, though dimmed somewhat by the moon, were still bright flecks of ice. The fields were shimmering. Only the hill, and the woods along the creek, were dark, like black onyx.

Paul reached the creek and stopped on the steel girder bridge. The water was black, the stars reflecting on the smooth surface. He could hear the rapids from further upstream. Feeling the bright coldness, he wished he could stay there for hours, gazing at the landscape of moonlight and shadow.

An animal rustled in the brush under the bridge. Paul thought of Father Dauwen's face filled with certainty, and blowing spirit clouds with his breath, he smiled at the night.

Blueline 7 (1985)

The Last Boy

On the TV screen, women wearing long printed skirts and beaded necklaces, trailing garlands of poppies, danced to music in a palm-tree-lined park. Not fiddling or country, which Paul had grown up with at the York Ferry Fourth of July barbecues, but rock and roll—a booming electric guitar beat which shook the fan-like fronds on the trees. The park was somewhere in California; he wished he were there, a link in that chain of weaving bodies, their faces uplifted in bliss, an almost religious ecstasy which might have had to do with drugs but which Paul preferred to believe was a natural product of freedom from order and adults.

He sipped his Genesee Cream Ale and switched off the TV when the "Summer of Love—1967" retrospective had ended, and the newsman started reciting numbers of dead troops, numbers of men missing in action—the daily body count in a place he didn't bother to locate on the colored metal globe in the living room. Vernon had served in the Air Force, but Paul knew nothing about his father's experience. It was a weekday, and the rest of the family was eating dinner at his grandmother's. Paul had managed to plead summer-school homework, and his mother, impressed, gladly took the others to Eleanor's house to allow him the silence in which to concentrate. Paul had never been much of a student, and the real reason for his desire to be alone was the case of beer he'd stolen that afternoon from behind the York Ferry Inn. Thrusting his head back, he poured the remaining contents of the bottle straight down. Beer number five. His twin, sister, and mother would return by about 9 o'clock or so, making it necessary for Paul to drink one and one-third six packs per hour to finish the entire case. His math, a least, was good for something. He pictured each beer bottle as a signpost he needed to pass on a journey whose destination was some idyllic place, complete with palm trees, girls in flowers, and the rock and roll which sounded so sensual he could almost caress the strands of music.

Without the television blaring, the Pinny farmhouse sat perfectly quiet in its cradle of valley, the nineteen acres of pasture stretching toward the low curtain of Madnan's Ridge to the west, Lake Champlain's bright blue visible in the east, his mother's gardens splashing the green landscape with multicolored vegetables and the brilliant yellow of sunflowers. Paul left the big window and followed the hall, stepping down when he passed into the addition; the farmhouse was like a rabbit hutch with new rooms added onto the original structure, one for the twins, one for Zoe Mae. ("A girl needs her privacy," Kay had said. Paul thought his sister's privilege clearly unfair.) The corridor sloped lakeward to the back bedrooms. He spied around his sister's things but found nothing of interest. Eleven-year-old Zoe Mae kept her room as neat as a military barracks, her favorite books stacked beside her bed. Underneath her pillow was the "hidden" flashlight, which everyone except Kay knew about, along with her two favorite books of the moment, *Harriet the Spy* and *The Long Secret*. Her bookcase was crammed with former favorites, which she still read constantly. If Zoe Mae liked a story, she would read it again and again until she could practically recite the words by heart. She often tried to keep the twins as captive audience, but they quickly grew tired of listening. At night, Zoe Mae read aloud to her imaginary sister, Ramona, who always remained attentive. After concluding there was nothing to distract him here, and no Ramona either, he shut her door carefully and leaned back to guzzle another Genny Cream.

His body felt warm and fluid, like those hippies in California must have felt. He smiled and swayed his hips, bumping the walls in an imitation of the dancers' movements as he made his way to the bathroom. Dancing and peeing at the same time, he misfired, and a puddle of urine formed on the floor. Oh, he felt good—a little sleepy, very content. He hoped to reach that same starry high that made the hippies' eyes flutter, but when he kneeled to wipe up the pee, a wave of nausea washed over him, and he fought the urge to vomit. After it passed, he stumbled out to his father's old tool shed, where Paul had established his hiding place for beer and other secrets.

A mirror in the shape of a jagged *P* which someone had long ago given his father lit the darkness with refracted sunlight, the Adirondack summer day still stretching on. Paul grinned at his reflection, and a sturdy round face returned the smile: big straight teeth and a head of thick curls, blue eyes with delicate lashes and amazingly acne-free skin. His build was still scrawny for thirteen, he thought, but consoled himself with the knowledge that everyone compared him to his brother Dean, his most charismatic sibling. Paul wondered what his father looked like now. Kay's only portrait of him was the U.S. Air Force shot of Vernon in his mechanic's fatigues, wrench in hand, a full-fledged acknowledgment of the camera in an expression that radiated pride, patience—even power. The picture, which hung in the living room so that it was the first thing one saw upon entering, was now twenty-five years old.

It seemed Vernon had engineered all the family photographs, appearing in none.

Surveying the ratchets and wrenches strung across the pegboard like a line of falling dominoes, Paul ran his fingers down the workbench. Coffee cans brimmed with nails, screws, and greasy, unidentifiable objects his father had called thingamabobs—Paul thought it was a real name until his mother corrected him. Vernon Pinny, in Paul's dim memory, was a tall man in overalls who puttered in this room late at night, his calloused hands in constant motion, his head bent to a task, fingernails black, one thumb permanently disfigured by a misplaced mallet blow. Paul was five when Vernon disappeared. The night before his father left for Canada, Paul and Joe fell asleep in Vernon's lap watching a TV special on the royal wedding of a month earlier. His mother had oohed and aahed, he remembered.

This shed, more than anyplace else on the property, had something of his father in it, some presence or spell, the smell of a man. Beneath a pile of drop-cloths, the remaining beer glistened; he took two more bottles. The room oozed darkness, things hidden and silenced. Mildewed cartons lined the back wall, none of them labeled. Once he'd investigated the top layer, finding only old magazines, bills, meaningless scraps of paper. Someday, Paul promised himself, he'd go through all of them and find something important, some key to his father his mother had overlooked. Maybe there were other photographs, mementos of Vernon's years in the Air Force, a helmet or a pair of boots. Maybe a medal, a letter of commendation. There would be no war letters, since Vernon hadn't met Kay until afterward, when he came home with his two broken legs.

Down the Short Bay Road in front of the house, a motorcycle flew, chrome glinting. Paul imagined himself racing down the Lakeshore Drive with no shirt on, the wind cooling his back, a keg of beer waiting at Elbow Beach. Himself as hero, a group of girls and guys greeting his arrival, crowding him in a crush of awe. He finished a Genny and grabbed another, making his way to the compost heap behind the kitchen. He thought he was clever by peeing directly into the pile, a gesture which would please his mother for its economy—life and death in a cycle and all that, blossoms growing from the dungheap. He was studying the ecosystem in school. Then he remembered Kay, in a flood of memory formerly suppressed, admonishing his father not to do that very thing. Urine kills things, she'd said. So Paul was destroying the heap of natural fertilizer beneath him, not supplementing it after all. He zipped up and pushed the thought away, letting the alcohol absorb it and all unpleasantness like a sponge expanding. He knew he was selfish to drink a whole case, to take all the pleasure for himself. Earlier he'd considered calling Kenny Heller, his best friend, to ask if he wanted to join him at the task, but had decided against it. Paul didn't want to share. He wanted to drink all of it, all by himself. Often he resented being a twin, being force to split everything in two. Tonight was a test he'd devised, a personal code of honor: to conquer a case of Genny single-handed without anybody knowing. "See, Mom—I *am* doing my homework," he said loudly and laughed.

Too bad he didn't have a cigarette, he thought suddenly, damning himself for not thinking ahead. He didn't like smoking cigarettes as much as smelling them. His father's Lucky Strikes burned perpetually on edges of counters, remembered at the last possible moment, caught in mid-air, his magician father's sleight-of-hand.

Stealing the case had been easy. George Reiser, owner of the Inn and Dean's father-in-law, was an old drunk who didn't get around to taking in his deliveries until after 9 in the morning. Paul had simply lifted a case off the top of the stack and hidden it in a nearby scrap wood pile, transporting the bottles in two separate trips on his bicycle, the beer out of sight in an IGA grocery bag. The summer school teacher had threatened to call his mother after Paul showed up an hour late, but he talked her out of it, claiming a flat tire had forced him to walk the full four miles. He smiled a lot, looked contrite, and told her repeatedly how sorry he was; could he stay after class and find out what he'd missed? She was a young woman from the college in Plattsburgh—not a local. She didn't call Kay after all.

Sun bathed Madnan's Valley in a last soft light of gold flecked with green. Paul remembered sitting on the porch at this exact time of evening and watching his father, shirtless beneath the faded blue overalls, as he tilled the garden with a spade. Sweat ran down his arms in muddy rivulets, and his sparse, straw-colored hair was matted to his head. He wore no hat, no garden gloves. He'd plant the spade in the loamy earth, jump on the metal edge to push it deeper, then pick up a mountain of soil and turn it over, inspecting the rich dirt with his work-calloused fingers. Then he'd straighten up and start again. The process went on forever, and Kay's two garden plots loomed for miles in Paul's memory. The sun had fallen across Vernon's shoulders as it dipped behind the ridge, striping the furrows with elongated triangles of light, and darkness closed in swiftly after that. His mother gathered the twins to put them to bed. "No," his father had called. "Wait! Let me hold the youngest a while; you take the other one in." Paul and Joe had sat on either side of his mother all evening watching Vernon dig, drinking lemonade, and Joe had fallen asleep. Why didn't Vernon call him by his name? And why was Joe "the other one"? It didn't make sense, yet it suggested why Paul had always known without understanding why, that his father preferred him in some odd way, that he was more interested in his youngest son. Paul was born second by a few minutes; his mother called him "the last boy." The last baby was Zoe Mae, and she said she couldn't remember anything about their father. She had no memory of him at all.

Stealing beer from the Inn became a habit. Paul couldn't believe how easy it was; anyone could have done it, but he saw no evidence that he had company in his thievery. Every morning he took the empties back, leaving them with the others behind the dumpster. He was depositing some bottles into the wooden Genesee crates when Eileen Reiser opened the back door and found him.

"Hey, Paul! What are you doing?"

"Oh—not much. Hi Eileen. I, uh, found these empties on Route 22, so I thought I'd drop them off over here to let you leave them for the delivery guy and that way, you'd get the deposit."

"That's awfully generous of you, but if they're not ours in the first place, you could just take them to the IGA and get some pocket money." Eileen was a petite blond girl with crazy, frizzy hair that reminded him of the dancing hippie women in California. She was smiling at him now (probably thinking he was a cute boy), so he figured she didn't suspect the theft.

"That's a good idea, but I'll just leave these here for now, 'cause I have to get home to water the garden before the sun gets too hot."

"You people really help each other out, don't you?" Eileen asked, braiding her waist-length hair to one side of her face, looking thoughtfully in the direction of the lake, which wasn't visible from the Inn. The farmhouse was out of sight as well, tucked behind the rise where the burnt-out remains of a general store still stood.

"Pretty much. Even my dumb twin."

"Don't call him that. Joe's a sweet boy."

"He's so boring, though. He never wants to do anything."

"Still. I thought you all stuck together."

"Oh, we do. I'm just fooling. Gotta go. See ya."

She waved at him before starting to heft the cases of Genessee and Budweiser bottles into the rear of the bar. Paul circled back, making a clean, graceful arc on his bike across the parking lot.

"Want some help with those?"

"Buddy, I've been lugging these things around since I was your age. Younger even." She wiped her hands on a cloth apron and held them up for inspection. "See?" They were red and cracked with use, dry from years of rinsing glasses, even though she was just eighteen. Paul was impressed.

"I wish I worked here."

"You do? Why on earth would you?"

"Oh, it seems like fun."

She laughed, hoisting a case onto her hips, and didn't object when Paul followed her inside, a case under each arm. "It's a lot of things, but it's not fun." She propped the beer against the wall, leaning her body into it as she opened the cooler door. "It's hard, hard work. You looking for a job?" Her words trailed over her shoulder to Paul, who was thrilled to be standing behind a bar for the first time. The collection of colored bottles and gleaming silver spouts looked like flasks in an alchemist's laboratory. "My dad's been talking about hiring someone to do a little extra cleanup—sweeping, mopping, that kind of stuff. It's off the books, of course. How old are you, anyway?"

"Almost fourteen."

"Well, I'll ask him about it, okay? When he gets up. You sure you're interested? It's just for the season, you know. We always have more business now— all the summer people and their guests. Dad thinks the place should be cleaner. It's better for business, he says."

"Listen, Eileen. Tell your dad I definitely want to do it."

For a moment she looked him over, a glimmer of suspicion in her eyes. "You're awfully eager. I didn't think pushing a broom around sounded so glamorous."

They were back outside, and she cocked her head at the upstairs window, as if she'd heard her name called. "Come back tomorrow, and I'll let you know what he says."

Summer school ended in late July—he barely passed—and Paul's days acquired a new rhythm. Each morning he spent two hours sweeping and mopping the York Ferry Inn, and the rest of the day was his own. Joe watered the garden while Paul sampled the various liquors of his employer. Each day he poured something different into his canteen, mixed it with water, and drank the results at the beach in the afternoon. His friends assumed he was drinking water, and Paul liked to think this was partially true; he didn't like to lie unnecessarily. After a few close calls, he learned not to drink too much—never again a case in three hours!—so that he didn't stumble or appear noticeably altered. Gum disguised his breath, and no one ever said a word. With luck and a little maneuvering, he avoided having to offer his canteen when a friend was thirsty. Paul felt at peace when he drank; he could actually pinpoint the precise moment when the alcohol infused his blood with tranquility, flushing his entire body with a slow solution of contentment.

At Elbow Beach, girls from school congregated near him and his friends, everyone's towels overlapping, their transistors all tuned to the same SUNY-Plattsburgh station which played the California music, the foreign names of the groups like the words of an incantation: Jefferson Airplane, Quicksilver Messenger Service, Grateful Dead, and his favorite, "It's a Beautiful Day."

He swam out to the raft on his first school-free day and lay there a long time, absorbing the brilliant heat of the sun, which failed to warm his heart, nor would it slow his rapid pulse, now quickened by the plunge into Lake Champlain's icy waters. He remembered learning in science class how the heart instinctively speeds up when someone senses danger—the example had been a deer seeing a lion in the distance. This fear caused the blood to pump faster, which enabled the deer to run faster than it could normally—to run for its life. The adrenaline of survival, his teacher called it. His own heart beat that fast, as if he, too, were running for his life, stock still on the bobbing raft. But what was he afraid of? He could see no predator stalking his scent, no enemy lurking in the shadows. Paul sat up and looked at the shore where his friends sprawled across blankets on the hard sand, some of the girls playing cards, one boy brazenly smoking a cigarette, the primary colors of their bathing suits like quilted patchwork under the deepening azure sky. Frieda, a farm girl who was a twin herself and a year older than he, waved at him vigorously, waved him back to shore.

"Hey Paul! Paul Pinny! Paul Pinny!"

It sounded like a chant, the syllables meaningless in such rapid succession. He saw his metal canteen, half-full of the alcohol solution, catching the sun's rays like a beacon, awaiting him on the towel beside Frieda, and swam toward it.

Nighttime always drew him to the shed, his father's lingering presence like the invisible magnet of the North Pole. He went late, after everyone had fallen asleep. The only side effect of alcohol, as far as he could tell, was raging insomnia. Though he never had hangovers, Paul could rarely get to sleep before dawn, so he used the early morning hours, when Joe was snoring loud enough for them both, to mine the contents of his father's old boxes. The first few weren't interesting at all—financial records of the last several years, some blurry pictures of his siblings, tied with string, carefully dated. Why didn't his mother throw these away? He found a cracked bowling ball that said,"Vernon Pinny, Top Scorer, 1955–6" in gold script letters. This surprised him. He couldn't remember his father doing anything like bowling in the York County Bowling League. He always remembered his father alone: alone in a room, a field, even in the auto shop, where his partner, Henry, always worked nearby. Paul discovered an old pair of Vernon's black-rimmed glasses, the lenses badly scratched. He tried them on and looked for his reflection in the jagged P, losing his balance immediately, dizzy from the magnification. He looked like a fish in a funhouse mirror, all bloated and wide. Was that how his father saw the world? As if from the inside of an aquarium? Probably not; Paul understood how prescription glasses were supposed to work. It was strange, though, to feel the heavy rims on his nose, to know that his mysterious father had worn them himself; they'd rested on his sharp cheekbones and circled behind his ears, framed the world his father knew. Paul pocketed the glasses, wondering again why his mother had not gotten rid of such useless things, although he was certainly pleased to have them. It seemed she had thrown nothing away.

All though August he worked his way toward the bottom of the pile, finding little of interest. There were documents about mortgages, paperwork from the York Ferry Garage, receipts and business correspondence. The auto repair shop his father had made prosper for fifteen years was now defunct; Henry had failed to maintain Vernon's high standards, or that was how his mother explained it. Dean had quit his apprentice position immediately after his father's disappearance. Paul sifted through inventory accounts, delivery notices from the Greyhound depot in Marysville. What could his mother be thinking to save all this junk? He kept looking. It was cold in the shed at night, so he always took a sweater, and had never gone barefoot after the first time, but still, a chill settled upon him under the bare bulb, and when he caught a glimpse of his reflection, it was dim and chalky. Of course he kept the curtains drawn tight so that no light would leak, curtains cut raggedly and sewn by his father from old Army blankets, now moth-eaten and tattered. Here, sometimes, he felt afraid, threatened by the cold, close air, by the lingering presence of his absent father, the smell that never faded—although he knew this sensation was the reason for his visits. The shed was little used; Dean had built his own workshop where he lived with his wife close to town. Steve had never been inclined to putter around in here, always preferring to be outdoors, even on the coldest of days. Neither was his twin interested enough to investigate. And his mother stayed away, except for storing her garden tools, and to add a box to the pile each year. It was just Paul and his father in here, the jagged mirror and the light bulb.

When the end of the season approached, Eileen told him they wouldn't need his help after one post-Labor Day cleanup. She would return to doing those tasks herself, and less frequently. "York Ferry people don't need their bars so clean," she told him. He couldn't tell if she was being sarcastic or not.

Paul worried about his alcohol supply getting cut off, but if he had the will, he would find a way—that's what his mother always said about solving problems. In his possession was a key to the Inn, which he would have to return to Eileen. No one had ever said, however, that he couldn't make a copy. Without too much hesitation, he biked up to the hardware store in Port Elizabeth to have it done. (The hardware lady in York Ferry knew everyone and always tried to guess what kind of locks the keys were for.) He resolved to be cautious, to come early in the morning and never to take too much; no one need ever know.

One windy night late in October, Paul reached the last box. He trembled as he carried it to the workbench, imagining some lost treasure inside, some precious token of his father previously overlooked. Although he usually limited his drinking to daytime, so that he was stable by dinner, when he would see his mother, that night he took the canteen to the shed. The cement floor leaked cold upward through the souls of his sneakers, and the jacket over his sweater failed to keep him warm. Lighting the woodstove tempted him, but the risk of discovery was too great. His breath fogged the air before him, clouding the mirror's flecked surface. After a swig on the canteen, he set to undoing the flaps of the carton, whose bottom was green with mildew and icy to the touch.

Junk. Another box of junk. Blank York Ferry Garage invoices, a catalogue of General Motors standard transmission parts, and a collection of poorly focused black and white snapshots of an infant spread-eagled across the braided rug in the living room. "Dean, first crawled, 1948" was printed on the back in a neat hand, each picture barely distinguishable from the one before it. There were birthday cards from Dean's first birthday and an envelope of recipes cut from the newspaper. When Paul lifted a *Time* magazine from 1946, it let fall an unsealed envelope. Inside was a yellow piece of paper covered with writing; it had to be his father's. His letters were narrow, at first staying well between the lines, but by the end of the page, the words overlapped and bled into the margins. Although many phrases had been crossed out, the letter seemed complete, awaiting only a signature. The date was Nov. 11, 1946. The address of the farmhouse was printed neatly in the corner of the envelope, but there was no addressee.

Irene,

I can't stop thinking about you no matter what I do. I've met a nice girl who I'm going to marry tomorrow, but I can't get you out of my head or out of my heart, and I'm thinking tonight I should call off this thing with Kay and come back to Antwerp. But I can't even send this letter. I do know, though, that I didn't want to leave you that morning, how I knew even before I stepped out your door that I'd never see your lovely face again, and it was either going AWOL or leaving you, and I left you, and I'll never forgive myself for losing you. Never and never. What's that saying—we won the war but lost the battle. I did lose you. Oh god, I did. I remember your shoulder blades, poking out from your sweet back like nubby wings, the firmness of your stomach beneath my hand, how small your palm was against mine, my fingertips overlapping yours a full inch. Oh Irene, how could I have shielded you from the Germans with their bombs? After surviving three years in the room with no windows, you were given the air, then had it taken from you. How could I believe in god after that? He didn't protect you. I didn't either. I will never forgive god, nor me.

Your,

It didn't say anymore, Paul assumed that was the end of the letter. Vernon needed only to sign it and send it. Paul read through the cramped words again and felt confused, wanting for himself the love his father harbored for this woman, this stranger. It was obvious to Paul that Vernon had gone in search of her, so many years later that even if she had survived the war, she probably wouldn't care about Vernon anymore. She probably had a family of her own. How many children would she walk away from to find Vernon? He felt his mother had been wronged, somehow, by this previous love; it was an intimate act of treason on his father's part. Paul should have found one love letter in all these boxes addressed to Kay and not some foreign girl who was probably dead.

"What the hell are you doing in here!"

His mother slammed the door behind her, wrapped in Vernon's old overcoat, wearing his black rubber fishing boots as if it were raining or muddy outside, but they were completely dry, dwarfing her short legs.

"What are you doing?" she repeated.

"I couldn't sleep, Mom. I just couldn't." He tried to measure her anger; she looked more worried than mad, a sign in his favor. "So I came in here to look around for a while."

Her gaze traveled the circumference of the room, noting his canteen, the open box, the magazine and piece of paper in his hand. The gray-blue of her irises and white of her eyes carried a strange, soft light into the room. Her hair was loose and disheveled, an airy cumulous cloud encircling her head. "Paul, it's freezing in here." She bit her lip. "I haven't been in the shed in a long time. Not at night." She looked again at the workbench, its surface covered with papers. "What are you doing, going through all that junk?"

"Just looking."

"Find anything?"

"Nope." He didn't know what to do with the letter, so he kept it in his hand while returning things to the box.

"Come on, son. You can clean up tomorrow. You scared me half to death when I couldn't find you in the house."

"Well, what were you doing up?"

"Sweetie, that's what I asked you, remember?"

Paul grabbed his canteen and tried to appear nonchalant as he slipped the letter beneath the magazine.

"Come on. You'll catch cold out here."

She pushed him out the door in front of her, and as she switched off the light, the bulb sizzled and sputtered out. He heard her murmur, "It almost smells like him in here."

In the warm, well-lit living room, she took his face in her hands and examined him closely. (He tried not to exhale.) He was just her height now, and growing still, so that she wouldn't be able to look him eye-to-eye much longer.

"Paul, is there something you're not telling me?"

He shook his head.

"Something at school? Your grades? You can talk to me. I won't get mad."

"Nothing, Mom. Really."

"Well, I don't like this, you roaming around in the middle of the night." Now that they were safe inside, Kay had recovered her anger. "You scared the hell out of me, you know, when I looked into your room, and you weren't there. And you weren't in the kitchen, or the bathroom. I got frantic. I just happened to glance out the window and see a tiny bit of light coming from the shed. Oh Paul," she said, stroking his hair rapidly and hugging him hard. "It was very odd, because for a minute—no, a split second, maybe—it was like when your father was here, and he could never sleep either, and he used to stay out there till all hours. I thought he was back. Or that it was a long time ago, and all these years hadn't happened."

Paul could feel his mother's heart beating through Vernon's overcoat, pumping against his own chest, and he remembered the deer's adrenaline, and then he couldn't tell if it was his own blood racing, or his mother's, or both. He didn't try to struggle out of her embrace, as he often did, and she whispered, "You miss him, don't you?"

He couldn't speak, but he nodded yes, yes he did.

Then she spun him around, slapped his cheek once, harshly, stinging him, and pushed him away. "Now don't ever frighten me like that again," she demanded, still whispering, but louder. "Do you understand?"

He didn't answer, and he didn't turn around but backed slowly toward his room, leaving her there in the center of the braided rug, empty-handed.

Blueline 13 (1992)

For Lack of a Road

The year 1930 was not a good year in the United States. Depression hovered darkly over the country and any change was usually for the worse. But residents in the sparsely settled Adirondacks had cause to rejoice. The state, after years of agitation, finally built a twelve mile stretch of highway linking the village of Raquette Lake and Blue Mountain Lake, making possible for the first time automobile travel from one to the other. Until then a traveler between the towns was forced to take a circuitous water route in summer or a rough sled road across the ice in winter.

The link would have been welcome when eight years earlier, in August 1922, Thomas Callahan Sr. died at Sagamore Lodge near Raquette Lake. Although his family was reconciled to a death that ended a long and useful life, they realized they would have a problem transporting the old gentleman to the family burial plot in Warrensburg, New York, about seventy miles to the southeast. However, the only road out of Raquette Lake led southwest. To reach the main road to Warrensburg they would have to take a choppy steamboat trip across Raquette Lake to Forked Lake, then travel a barely passable corduroy road to the paved highway. Theresa, the youngest daughter, thought it would be more dignified to take the train from Raquette Lake, but the train went in the opposite direction.

"Good Lord, Theresa, it would take two days to go that way with train connections so poor," her brother Maurice pointed out. "It's two hundred miles out of the way. We'll go by the lake." The others agreed with him in spite of Theresa's stiff displeasure.

After a funeral service at Sagamore Lodge, the sons and grandsons of the old man lifted the coffin carefully onto the mail wagon drawn by the big bay team Ned and Dave, whose tendency was always to go as fast as possible along the bumpy four mile track to Raquette Lake Village. Simons, the wizened little driver, had trouble controlling them. He felt his customary method, a whiplash of loud curses, was somewhat inappropriate. Thomas' widow, Ellen, his four sons, three daughters and the grandchildren, uncomfortably warm in their black mourning garments this August day, jiggled along behind in a string of carriages. The dry dust of the road, thrown up by the horses' feet, settled on the riders, and the sun shone down hot and bright.

The big excursion steamer was at the dock and the coffin was lowered on deck while the family got aboard. After maneuvering the various automobiles, which had been parked in the village, onto a large float attached to the steamboat, they were ready to depart.

The boat started off with a blast of its whistle. About an hour later it arrived on the other side of the lake where the undertaker met them and slipped the coffin into the shiny black hearse while the men unloaded the cars. The procession limped slowly along the rough road from Forked Lake to the highway that would eventually lead them to Warrensburg.

As they passed through villages along the way, friends and relatives joined the funeral cortege, dressed in their somber mourning clothes. In North Creek the sleek hearse chugged unexpectedly to a halt. "Hell!" exploded the driver. Family members sighed resignedly. A dog sauntered over to study his reflection in the shiny ebony finish of the hearse, while mechanics from the local garage huddled under the heavy hood tinkering with the motor. After a restless wait of nearly an hour, the repairs seemed successful, and the procession moved on. Just outside the cemetery, the hearse shuddered and stopped again. Theresa mentioned that if they had gone by train they wouldn't have had to worry about breakdowns. The family carried Thomas Callahan the rest of the way by foot, and as gently as possible laid him to rest. He was the only one so privileged.

It was late afternoon and a cooling wind had risen. John, the oldest son, felt that now their spiritual duties had been taken care of, their bodies could use some refreshment. "We'll have dinner before we start back," he said. But Theresa, always stoic, assumed that they would start back immediately and protested any delay. Some of the others, anxious to reach home, agreed with her, but some, not so stoic, were hungry. Family and friends shifted around trying to decide what to do. Finally they agreed to have dinner in the hotel before starting for home.

It was dark when they reached Forked Lake and they shivered as they emerged from the warm cars into the chilly night air. Half obscured by fog, the steamboat was waiting for them at the dock. John settled his mother and the others in the cabin, then went up on deck. He whistled with dismay when he saw how dense the fog was. Navigation would be difficult on the big lake, which could be treacherous at times, with hidden rocks and shoals. They had to make their way through rocks at Needle Point, always hazardous. Maurice, piloting the steamboat, grimly handled both the boat and the advice from the passengers.

"Better go left here."

"There's a little rock over to your right."

"Port! Port!"

With the help of the chief engineer, who was operating the big twin screws in response to Maurice's signals, they finally landed safely on the other shore. In the cabin Theresa was saying that if they had started earlier the fog would not have been so bad.

Everyone was glad when they disembarked at the village of Raquette Lake and climbed stiffly into the carriages for the last leg of their trip. That day they had traveled a total of nearly one hundred and sixty miles by carriages, boat and car. It was a weary party that reached Sagamore Lodge just before dawn.

Ellen Callahan, sad, and worn from the long trip, took her hat off and rubbed her tired head.

"They keep talking about that road they are going to build between Raquette Lake and Blue Mountain Lake," she said, "but they don't seem to do anything but talk. An awful thing it is to have to go so far to be buried."

When Ellen herself died in 1932 the road was finished. Completed in a time of economic uncertainty, the road insured that progress in the central Adirondacks continued. It linked villages, shrank distances, eased the tedious business of burial. Yet less than fifty years later the familiar cortege of slow-moving vehicles bound for a distant cemetery is showing signs of becoming a ritual of the past, not for lack of roads but for lack of fuel. Recently an advertisement appeared in a New York newspaper urging people to buy final resting places in a new high-rise mausoleum in the city, rather than travel far afield for interment. "You can't get to Heaven in a limousine because the Lord don't sell no gasoline," the ad chants.

Ellen Callahan might have agreed. "If it is always going to be so hard to get there, the Lord better move Heaven a little closer to home."

Blueline 1, no. 1 (1979)

The Apple Orchard

Man fell with apples and with apples rose,
If this be true; for we must deem the mode
In which Sir Isaac Newton could disclose,
Through the then unpaved stars, the turnpike road,
A thing to counterbalance human woes.

—Byron

Some of my memories rise like bass, slapping the surface of the deep black pond with tails that live behind my eyes. They erupt quickly, gracefully descending into the depths of the past. Sometimes, though, I can freeze the frame; the edges of the slippery, soft-focus visions become diamond hard. The memory is tangible. I can pin it on the wall of my mind like a poster.

If I could rise from this bed where I now pass too few sleeping hours I would hop down the wooden back porch steps. I was a child, a girl, a young woman, when the summer morning promised sun and a swim in the pond. Barefoot, I would walk across the cinemascopic valley and begin to climb the endless hills that circle my home in the state of New York. Its famous city skyline pales in comparison.

The closer I get to the top, the more the sun burns the clouds; the maples blaze and mingle with the cherry and ash trees. The limbs creak and sway, gently brushing each other. I look up at the ceiling of entangled leaves and feel safe under the fresh green umbrella.

The camera of the mind shoots from many angles. Even though my body is brittle and dry I can see the past as well as the wild turkey can see the hunter. My ears wiggle and twitch. My voice, once a melodiously sculpted soprano, is now no more beautiful than the cackle of an old hen. My lifeline is dangerously frayed, but my mind is sharper than a city cat's eye; I remember.

Between muscle twinges and wheezes of the lung I review my life on paper which sucks ink from pen like a blotter. A woman from the county comes three times a day to bring me food and tend to other personals. I think she is not a full-fledged nurse, but she comes to my house and checks to see that I have not died in the middle of the night. I don't know how all this evolved to tell the truth, but here I am, in the same house where I was born, with a behind that needs to be wiped.

We are not friends and I'm afraid she will find my writings, for sometimes

I fall asleep and the notebooks are strewn on the bed. When I sleep it is deep and the sound of her laughter may not waken me. I don't mind her coming in my house, and, after these many months, have forgotten that it is, after all, her job. She clips my toenails. Can you imagine that?

Here is a memory as clear to me as the view from the parlor window:

Look across the north field of this upstate New York hill. See the tiptops of the apple trees bending in the wind? And Father's coffin sliding down the hill, bouncing through the orchard until finally it halts hard against my favorite apple tree? It still produces the sweetest of all the apples from the orchard, crispy enough to make your teeth cold, while the juice pours down your chin.

How many apples, I wonder, have I eaten in my life? One a day, certainly, for almost eighty years, if you count sauce, cider and pies. Sometimes people from upstate New York are called apple knockers, and I guess I know why. Even the dogs in this region love them. I've never had a dog that didn't grab the biggest apple on the ground between his paws, gleefully nudging it with his prune black nose. Then, tired of the apple ballgame the dog begins to nibble at the skin, breaking into its juice, finally tossing it down like a whiskey-drinking man.

Probably you were not there the day we tried to bury Father next to my brother Billy under the apple trees on the hill. Once in a while someone here-abouts with a sense of humor will still mention Will Leahy's funeral. He him-self would have had a good laugh and for the last forty or fifty years, so have I.

Soon after we found him dead in the barn, my mother and I carried Father into the house. Then, her skin the color of coal ashes, Mother sent me down the road. Dimly I understood that one rule of death in the country demands that the body be tended before it stiffens or it can't be laid out in a nice, tidy way.

Her voice was brittle and I saw no sign of tears when she said to me, "Irene, you go to Mrs. Dalton and tell her what's happened here. Mr. Dalton will build the casket tonight." She scribbled some numbers on a piece of paper and handed it to me.

"He'll need your father's measurements," she explained.

She spoke each word as if it would not take meaning unless I heard each vowel and consonant. I said nothing, but turned like a cloud and slowly left the house, hitching Gypsy as fast as my numb, blood-drained fingers could manage.

I waited at the Dalton place with the cotton-headed sense that the single most private act possible between two people was occurring between my parents. Still, the rules of tradition allowed that a neighbor, not a teenage daughter, would help to wash and dress the body. While I sat motionless at the Dalton's kitchen table, Mrs. Dalton saddled her little pinto and went to be with my mother.

It took more than half of the day to build the pine coffin, because Mr. Dalton took extra time padding it with horse hay and lining that with a soft white material. Left alone in the strange kitchen, I cradled my head on the table and escaped into sleep. I was as startled as a bird to feel Mr. Dalton's soft hand on my shoulder. Those few empty moments before the reason I was there slammed me awake were precious and fleeting.

When finally we loaded the box onto the wagon, I heard the church bell in the distance. My father was thirty-eight years old and thirty-eight times the bell tolled.

"Do you want me to take you back, Reeni," Mr. Dalton asked gently, but this was to be my contribution to Father's funeral. The tolling of the church bell signaled a release and I could not see through my tears. Even Gypsy seemed sad, but the horse knew her way, and brought me and the coffin home.

It took a day or two for the farmers and their wives to get to our house. They came in wagons and on horseback, laden with baskets of food and sympathy. Just about everybody from our town and lots of people from surrounding hamlets came to pay their respects. The kitchen was filled with the women, all in bonnets and dark long dresses, sometimes forgetting to hush their tones. By this time my mother's face was round and red from crying, and the braid usually so tightly wound on top of her head was crookedly loose. She refused to move from Father's desk, testing the neighbor women's abilities to divert her.

As each failed one by one: "Come, Virginia, you must eat something," I watched my mother swell like a blowfish, ready to burst with the grief of her loss. I myself sat in a taciturn lump on a bench in the kitchen, waiting for the misery to end. Each minute passed in slow motion. Years later I wondered why I didn't take sad little Jacky and hide out in the fields. The old border collie's eyes were glazed with confusion; she would die of her own grief four days later. I buried her, wrapped in one of Father's flannel shirts, with the rest of my dead family.

Outside, men with faces covered in not necessarily clean beards meandered in small groups, talking quietly on the porch, shaking their heads. Even now, thinking about it, I gasp for air like a hooked carp: the waving motion of those people in our house, their faces drifting back and forth over my face, into my eyes, and my mouth and nose like water lapping a wrecked ship on the beach. They took my breath away.

The ladies took command and directed the burial day with hands of experience. When it was time, one of them told the men to hitch up. Looking like sheepish little boys, they hoisted the pine coffin onto the wagon.

October is a capricious month in this part of the country and too many changes can make any animal nervous and irritable. That week the weather had turned from hot and steamy to wet and chilly. Just as we stepped into the wagon, a cold breeze blew up, grabbing at our hats and hair.

Gypsy, normally a calm horse, was skittish and so were the men, for more than one grave had been dug around our town. Most of the burials had been predictable—World War I killed thousands of soldiers from the country. But no outside influences had killed this man, just a lifetime of hard work.

Who determined that Mother and I should ride the burial wagon up the hill to our family plot was a mystery to me, but it turned out to be a bad decision. As we neared the top of the hill where Rev. Moore—an Episcopalian that Mother believed to have secret Catholic liaisons—was leading hymns, a small cyclone roared across the field. Young apple trees genuflected while the women struggled to keep their skirts over their legs.

Branches twisted and cracked like brittle bones. Mother and I held onto the seat which was fastened only well enough to keep us both from crashing backward. Father's brother, Uncle Alton, was busy trying to drive the horses when suddenly Gypsy whinnied and reared, raising the wagon perpendicular to the ground. Father's coffin slid, lurched, and slid again like a waxed sled. Everyone else had walked up the hill in front of the wagon; no one was behind to divert the runaway pine box. As it gathered momentum, it bounced and rolled, scraped and slid to the bottom of the hill, lodging against the best apple tree on the farm. Though later people said otherwise, the coffin did not break open.

"Irene!" my mother screeched between hysterical screams, which caused Gypsy to gallop as if she'd been stung by a yellow jacket. Mother wailed, grabbing at her throat and the air. While Uncle desperately tried to control the horse, I wrapped my arms around my mother's rounded shoulders, hugging her face close to my breast, whispering, I think, that "it" would be all right. We lurched back and forth, melded together in a frenzy of motion. It was scant protection. In the process my bouncing elbows knocked her best bonnet, her eyeglasses, and anything else that was not attached directly to her, under the wheels of the buggy. By the time Gypsy had torn loose from the hearse, blood spurted from Mother's split lip and my jaw was achingly blue.

For the solitary moment in time when we were one, I could feel her heart pounding on top of mine. We panted the same air together in short rhythmic breaths, as if the umbilical cord still pulsed between us.

The story of Father's funeral grew to gruesome proportions over the years. Contrary to rumors which still exist and skewed the truth of Father's burial day, we did not call it off altogether. When it became clear that neither Gypsy nor the wagon were in a condition to continue up the hill, a few men carried the coffin. They took the time to nail the boards and secure the top while Mother and I, disheveled and dirty, walked to the gravesite. I heard the hollow pounding of hammers. Gypsy, running haywire somewhere down in the valley, whinnied crazily.

When we reached the grave, Mother took both of my hands and looked me in the eye. The rough wind gusted again, played with our skirts. Apples thudded to the ground all around us and suddenly my mother smiled. The strain of the day had stripped us both, and giggles erupted slowly until we were roaring with laughter; until tears flowed like rivers down our cheeks.

Father would have approved.

Blueline 16 (1995)

Good Ol' Granny

On my birthday Granny gave me one of Gramp's fly rods and showed me some of the basics in the driveway. I liked the barrel roll cast the best, and wanted to try it in the river in front of the house right then, but she'd told me to wait—anticipation was the greatest part of fishing, patience, too—something I didn't have much of that summer when I was twelve.

At four-thirty the next morning she pushed open the door to Gramp's bedroom where I lay, already awake, listening to the river. "Come on, Sam. Time to get up." She waited till I had my feet over the edge of the bed, and when I looked up, she winked. "We'll see if old George wants to play today," she said.

I'd of given my new pair of sneakers to catch George and she knew it. Granny caught the big brown once or twice each summer on flies she tied herself. She'd stand in the middle of the river two or three early mornings each week, the tops of her waders hidden beneath a flowery patterned house dress. If he wasn't interested she'd walk downstream and catch and release the stocked rainbows and browns the state put in two or three times a summer for the tourists. Today I wouldn't be a spectator sitting on the bank, waiting to fish behind her with a can of worms in my back pocket. I put on my new Converse sneakers, a T-shirt, and slid down the banister.

"Good morning, Granny. I'm ready."

"Eat your cereal and toast," she said. "I'll put on my waders and we'll be ready."

I ate my cereal and watched the early morning mists on the river. From the front porch outside the window the river was within "twice spitting distance" Gramp always used to say. When I was younger Granny would give me a sauce pan and I'd go down on the smooth round rocks when the river was low and scoop up tiny minnows. Against the white enamel of the pan, I could see their skeletons flex as their forked tails pushed them around. I drank the cereal milk and put the dishes in the sink, deciding Granny's ideas about anticipation didn't do much for me.

She was tying a fly onto her line in the garage where she'd put her fly-tying vise and materials after Gramp had passed on a couple years ago. She handed me a tiny royal coachman and said, "Tie this on like I've shown you."

"What are you using?" I asked.

"This green and white one. George went for it two years ago about this time of year." On the bench was the small spiral notebook where she logged every catch of George she'd made.

"Do you think I have a chance, Granny?"

"How many fisherman do you see fishing this stretch every summer?"

"Lots." I ran the tippet through the eye, twisted the line three times and threaded the end into the loop above the eye, then snipped off the end.

"George is as cantankerous as your grandfather. As particular, too," she said. She stepped into the light by the garage door, grey-green waders against a paisley print dress. "Fisherman's luck doesn't have anything to do with catching George," she said. "Every offering must be perfect."

I followed her to the river, and we entered the water just below the house. Every spring I helped her and Gramp clear a rough sandy path among the slippery river rocks; this year I'd done it myself. The path went from one flat or slanted rock to another, and from atop or behind these she cast into the pool where George lived; long, arched casts that silently, gracefully placed the fly wherever she chose. Mists curled around the bottom of her dress as she stepped up onto the first rock and stripped line. "Be quiet," she said in a whisper. "There's two of us." She held three loops of line between pursed lips and put the fly in motion. Ten, fifteen, twenty feet, the fly flew softly back and forth from the tip of her rod. When the line she fed through her lips was all in the air, she followed through and the fly settled on the water above the big rock where George lived. "Anybody home?" she whispered, and watched the fly drift. Nothing. My hands squeezed the cork handle of my rod, and I stared, willing a fish to rise to the fly. She retrieved the line and gathered the coils between her lips. This time she cast to the left in slower water, then barrel-rolled the line out toward the big rock. I followed her to the next rock nearer the center of the river. "C'mon out and play, George," she said. "Show my grandson your mettle."

I'd always wondered what she was saying as I saw her lips move from where I sat on the river bank. She's tempting him, I thought—coaxing him to the fly—the same way she talked to the dominoes when she was losing.

At the next rock she reached into the front pocket of her dress and removed a red and green fly from a piece of sheep's wool. "Tempting, isn't it?" she asked, and held up the fly for me to see. I nodded, and wanted to ask when it would be my turn. We were now on the far side of the river, and she switched the rod to her left hand so the backlash didn't catch in the balsam trees; their smell reached us as the first heat of day began to break the mist. She let the fly land directly above the big steep-sided rock and fed slack. The fly sucked into and under the current. "He's not interested today, Sam." She brushed her free hand through her blue-white curls, then scratched behind her right ear. "Maybe he's gone girlin'," she said, and smiled, gathering a loop between her lips. She cast once more, then hooked the fly to the metal clasp on her rod and told me to give it a try.

I really mucked it up, whipping the water as soon as I had ten feet of line out. The fly slapped into the water a long ways from where I intended. George, if he was anywheres near, must've thought a whole gang of city slickers was up there thrashing around. Granny offered instructions, but I was so nervous I couldn't do anything right; it had seemed so easy in the driveway.

"Rest," she said, after ten minutes. "You're all worked up." She chuckled. "Sam, instead of buck fever, you've got fish fever, I declare." She patted my head, and told me she wished Gramp was here to see us. "We'll go down to the faster water where your delivery won't matter so much. Maybe you can catch some of the stockers."

We walked back the way we had come, and on the bank she pulled apart her rod and rested it against a tree. "I'm not going down too far," she said. "Beverly is taking me to Westport to see the dentist this afternoon, and I've got to make a raspberry pie for the bake sale before she comes."

I led the way down the path, trailing my fly rod behind me. I'd fished this stretch with worms, but today I felt like I did the day I moved from pee wee to little league baseball. The fly rod was light as a toothpick, and no worm can bulged in my back pocket. I worked my way out into the river and cast. Granny told me to hold my elbow in more, and worked down the river with me on the bank. "Hold the rod straight up," she said, above the rush of water against the rocks. "Try to put it in that quiet water over there." I looked to see where she pointed, but I couldn't do it. The line bellied out in the current and dragged the fly away. I worked over closer to her. "I'm doing everything wrong, Granny. Not even a stocker."

"By season's end you'll be fine," she said. "How long did it take to cast worms where you wanted? Think of that."

I sat down on a rock near where she stood. "I don't know, but I caught chubs the first time I went with Gramp."

"Keep practicing," she said. "I've got to get busy with that pie. If you get hold of one remember to keep the tip up."

I fished down to the bridge and tried to visualize everything she did. In the shadow of the bridge a four-inch chub inhaled the fly and I thought I'd hooked into George's brother. The fly rod tip bounced and dipped and I almost fell down twice before I finally lifted the chub out of the water. I must be getting better, I thought, as I walked back along the shore to the big rock.

I cast from the bottom of George's pool. After a while my shoulder began to ache and I changed flies. A black gnat didn't work either. When I gave up, I waded to the rock and tried to drive him out with my feet. But if he was there he didn't budge. Maybe tomorrow.

A peanut butter and peach jam sandwich was ready when I got back. For my dessert Granny had made a small raspberry pie from the leftover crust and berries.

"Beverly will be here soon," she said. "Want to ride along?"

"No thanks. I'll mow the lawn and go swimming."

"That's nice," she said. "You didn't catch George?"

"No. Just a chub. But I didn't get skunked."

"Practice some more in the yard. Aim straight."

I was mowing the lawn down by the road when my mother drove up. I shut the mower off and walked over. "Sammy," she said, "there's been an accident. Your grandmother was hurt pretty bad. Get in the car." I got in, slammed the door, and Mom took off. She told me that halfway to Westport Granny decided her door wasn't shut tight. Mom explained the door opened the opposite way on Beverly's foreign car, and the wind sucked Granny out when she opened it.

"How bad is she hurt, Mom?"

"I don't know. Beverly was very upset when she called."

They wouldn't let us see her. Beverly told Mom she'd held onto Granny's arm and slowed the car down to maybe thirty before she couldn't hold her anymore. Beverly was crying so hard Mom had to keep stopping her and repeating questions. It sounded like Granny had hit the pavement once, then rolled over and over in the ditch. Beverly told us she helped Granny get back in the car, but when Granny realized Beverly was heading to Westport to the closest doctor, she made her turn around and head back to Elizabethtown to her own doctor. "She screamed at me when I wouldn't turn around," Beverly said, "and there was blood all over."

The doctor came out and told us it was amazing that she hadn't broken anything. He said Granny had landed on her knees and elbows and was all scraped up; she'd be sore for quite a while. He took Beverly by the arm. "She told me about making you turn around. She's one tough lady."

Mom and I went to visit every day, and at night I went with Dad after supper. Granny complained about the food. We brought her milkshakes and candy bars. After four days they let her walk with a cane.

Mom and I stayed with her when she went home. She sat on the porch reading *Redbook* and *Family Circle* and looked at the river often. Mom was at the stove one afternoon making cookies and I was mowing the lawn when I saw Granny walking toward the river with her cane. I ran over and tried to help. "Go get your fly rod," she said. "I can't fish, but I can teach you how from the bank."

She told me exactly what to do: where to stand, how much line to let out, how to grip the rod and hold my arm. She told Mom not to worry about her falling. "Like the doctor said, I'm tough, and I'm not going to sit on the porch for the rest of the summer."

The next morning we were up at four-thirty. Granny let me help her to the bank above George's rock. "Ease out there quietly." She pointed to a spot thirty feet above the rock. "Wait. Let me tie this on for you." She snipped off a brown dun and tied on a red, yellow, and white fly. "That's a Granny special," she said. "Ought to at least make him come out for a look." She leaned against a tree. "Put it ten feet above the rock, Sam. Let it drift." She whistled when I reached where she wanted me to start casting.

She was right. On the first cast George lifted from the bottom and nudged the surface next to the fly. He looked like the chunk of railroad rail my grandfather used to straighten nails on. I rubbed sweat off my forehead, retrieved the fly, and put it in motion. Granny had her hands clamped together and stood on her tiptoes leaning against the tree. She motioned for me to cast a little left of the first spot. I whipped the water in back of me and saw her grimace as the fly slapped the water close to the rock. She motioned to the bank.

"George is interested," she said. "You've got to help me out there. At least to where I can get one good cast." She started down the bank. "Leave the rod here for now and put your arms around my waist." She kicked off her shoes, and by the time we got to the first rock she'd stubbed her bare toes twice. I knew it must hurt her ribs where I held her, but she didn't say anything. She rested on the rock while I got the rod, and smiled when I handed it to her.

"C'mon, George," she said. "Good ol' Granny has come to play." She made a practice cast off to the side, and pulled the fly away from an interested chub. She'd said one good cast, but it wasn't till the third one that George cooperated. I didn't think she had the strength to hold him. Her face was solemn as she gave line and let him dive in front of the rock. When he headed home she put tension on the line and led him away from the rock's sharp sides. "C'mon, George. That's a good fellow." For five minutes she followed him with the rod tip, the line z'ed back and forth, and her upper arm muscles bulged with effort. "Come over here, George. That's it."

I waded closer to her. "Good ol' Granny got you all tuckered out. Doesn't she, George?" George wagged his head half-heartedly against the hook's tension and finned in the current. "Take a good look at him, Sammy." She laid the rod down next to her and gripped the line. Hand over hand she drew George closer until she could reach into the water and stroke his back and sides. "Look, Sammy. He's almost asleep. Go ahead. Feel how smooth and firm he is."

But when I touched him above the dorsal fin he rolled and fought the hood. "Whoa," Granny said. "Whoa. Only used to my touch, I guess." George calmed down. His jaws moved slowly up and down.

"He's smart. Isn't he, Granny?" I said.

"Mind of his own," she said. "Takes a lot to fool him." She winked. "Like an old lady who forgot which way the car door opened." She gently released the hook from George's mouth, and gripped my shoulder tightly as we watched him swim downstream, like a tired fighter going home.

Granny paused at the river's edge and leaned against me. "You'll catch him some day, Sammy," she said. "You've just got to practice, do your best, and try to remember all you can."

"I will, Granny." I looked down at my grass-stained, muddy sneakers, and it seemed like such a long time since they'd been clean and white. I couldn't help myself from asking, "Do you think I might catch him tomorrow?"

Blueline 16 (1995)

The Man Who Loved Peonies

When I told Papa that I planned to marry Frank Johnson, he didn't say a word. He finished his glass of buttermilk in one long swallow and slipped out the kitchen door.

"Come back here and get dressed," I yelled. But he was already gone. He runs fast for a seventy-year old man. He disappeared around the corner of Wood Street, his blue bathrobe flipping in the wind.

By the time I found him the Moravian church bells were playing. He was at the quarry, under a mulberry tree, flicking pebbles with his thumb and forefinger. He'd pitch one and then grab the mulberry trunk with his left hand, leaning forward, craning his neck so he could see the stone hit the water. It makes me dizzy to stare straight down into the water like that. The surface is always dark and still.

The wind rattled the mulberry leaves; my eyes circled the top of the quarry wall. It was Sunday and I was glad the cement mills were quiet. Nazareth is a cement mill town. Portland Cement, Hercules Cement, Penn-Dixie Cement, Nazareth Cement. This quarry belongs to Lone Star Cement. I work for Lone Star. I weigh the Euclids when they come out of the quarry. I was the first woman in Local #677. When I first joined they had me stand all day watching the limestone crushers. It felt like my kidneys had come unglued, but I stuck it out. Before that I was a secretary for five years, even though my fingers weren't made for typing. I'd rather feel metal or grease any day. I like the scale house okay. It's boring, but I get to see Frank about once an hour, and I like the trucks, I like the smell of diesel fuel. I read mysteries and listen to the radio. I can tell Frank's rig by the sound of its engine, by the whine, and by the way he shifts. He's smooth with the clutch. He loves that truck.

When he stops at the scale house he'll hop down to hug me. We'll smile and kiss, and Frank will shove his hands into the back pockets of my coveralls. I push him away and tell him to drive carefully. Things have a way of falling into the quarry. Two years ago Tom Ratliff went over the edge in his rig. It was another old quarry, filled with water. The divers pulled him out, but that big Euclid is still down there.

When I was seven my brother David dove into an old quarry and drowned. All the kids swam back there then. No one cared. We jumped off ledges, floated on inner tubes. We flapped our arms wildly as we fell into the water. David pounded his chest and yelled like Tarzan. Someone dared him to dive from the top of the wall and he did.

He never came up, and I haven't been swimming since that day.

That was the day Papa began sitting at the quarry, looking over the water, looking up at the sky, looking, just looking. Then Mom filed for a divorce and left the state. Papa says I have eyes like my mother. "Wild eyes," he says. We keep pictures in the hallway. My favorite is the one with my mother as Miss VFW. She's handing Papa a trophy for Northampton County Yodeling Champ. She's kissing him on the cheek. One time I took the picture down to clean the glass. Papa very calmly told me to put it back. "It's clean enough," he said.

Papa hardly ever yodels anymore, but his peonies are another story. He lives for the week they're in bloom. He has red peonies, pink peonies, white peonies; his favorite is the white with the red center. I have heard their names since I was a child. Emma Klehm, Sarah Bernhardt, Felix Crousse, Charlie's White, and Festiva Maxima. "They're from the old country," Papa says. "They can't be bought."

We have peonies everywhere; and when they bloom, the fragrance is as thick as a morning fog. The smell hangs in the air.

The wind raked through the mulberry leaves again. Papa pitched another stone over the quarry wall. I glanced up at the hard green berries. "Papa?" I scratched at the dirt with a twig and waited for Papa to look at me. "Frank bought a new Peterbilt yesterday. He wants me to be his partner. He says we can haul sides of pork from Des Moines to L.A." I pinched the dirt between my fingers and sifted it. "He's going to teach me to drive. And he says that in five years we'll have enough saved for a down payment on a house."

"Five years is a long time," Papa said. He flipped another pebble over the wall and leaned forward. As I grabbed his bathrobe, he jerked his head around. "A day is a long time."

"Come on Papa," I said. "Let's go home."

"Let's," he said. But he didn't budge. So we sat there. I leaned back against the tree and watched the clouds stretch over South Mountain. I closed my eyes and listened to Papa ramble on about one last frost in May. When I realized I was listening to the traffic on Rt. 22, and not Papa, I jumped up. He had slipped off his bathrobe and was unbuttoning his pajama top.

"That's enough, Papa."

"It's not," he said. His shirt dropped to the ground and he stood at the edge of the wall, legs spread, arms raised in a diving pose.

"Would you please, please—"

He glanced over his shoulder at me.

"Put your clothes back on."

Papa laughed, a short, quiet laugh, and when he looked back over the wall I grabbed his pajama bottoms and pulled him to the ground. "Now that's enough." I held out his robe.

"Water's too cold yet anyway." He clapped his hands and his arm curved and shot into the air like a diver. His eyes brightened, and then he stopped suddenly, as if he'd heard something. I listened to his breathing, to the leaves in the wind. I stared at the single deep line in his forehead and thought how funny it looked, sloping downward from his left eye toward his right. It made his head appear to be cocked to one side. As I moved closer I saw my reflection in his eye. Papa gave me a puzzled look, and then kissed me on the temple.

He slipped into his bathrobe, and I wished he could just fly. I wanted to let him go. I wanted him to wander in the quarries with a bouquet of peonies in each hand. But last month they set off a blast when he was less than fifty yards from the wall. Papa was still laughing when I picked him up in the office after work. He couldn't hear a thing, and his hands made great circular motions in the air, like a cloud from an atomic blast. "Something has to be done before he gets hurt," the supervisor told me.

Papa was quiet as we walked back to the house, and when we got to the yard, he kept pausing, sliding his fingers over the petals. After lunch he went out to work with his flowers. I helped. He'd stop every minute or so and bury his face in a mass of blossoms. "Be careful," I said. "You'll get bitten by an ant." Our neighbor sprays his bushes as soon as the buds appear. Papa says, "He'd better not kill my ants."

In the eighth grade I asked my biology teacher why ants crawled over peony buds. To drink the nectar, he said. When I told Papa, he nodded, "That makes sense." Papa would yodel for my friends, and he'd give them each a bunch of peonies, and they'd say, "Your father is crazy."

It wasn't long until St. Regis Paper forced him to retire. He had mixed glue for thirty years, white glue that smelled like ripe cider. They gave him a cheap watch and a citation for his service and sent him home. "Fine," Papa said. "I'll have more time to tend to my flowers." But that glue had burned up his brain.

My Aunt Helen, Papa's sister, says it wasn't the glue. She says my grandfather was the same way. A real simpleton. I wonder if this is what I have to look forward to when I get old. It scares me to think of having kids. Frank says that is okay. He says we'll just run that semi until we're gray. Frank is the only man who likes me in coveralls.

Papa was on his hands and knees, spreading the leaf-mulch tight against the base of the plants. He kept saying, "It's too cold for May, too cold."

"Would you quit worrying."

"Easy for you to say."

When we went back into the house Papa took out all his spiral notebooks. His weather books. He writes down the highs and lows for each day. And he has counted the rainy days in December, the snows in January, the fogs in February, the cloudy days in March, and the sunny days in April—for years. "There's a pattern to all this," he says. "If a man could just figure it out." He knows that when the buds are too tight in April they won't open in time for Memorial Day. Or when it's too warm in March, they'll blossom quickly and die.

As I peeled potatoes for dinner, Papa leafed through his notebooks, and from time to time he'd call out, "June!" That's my name, and so I'd holler back, "What?" But he didn't answer, and when I listened closer I heard him calling out the months. "March. April. May. June." Whenever he said "June," it was the final word and he said it fast and loud, like some kid playing one, two, three, redlight.

"June!" His voice lowered. He was calling me this time.

I covered the potatoes, dried my hands and went to the living room. "What is it?" I said.

"It's just like '65," Papa said. "Look."

That was the year David died and I didn't want to look. I remembered how spring came in February and the peonies were burned by a late frost.

Papa was on the floor, with notebooks scattered from the end table to the television. "The difference is one frost," he said.

"Would you clean up in here?" I picked up a few papers, straightened them, and added, "Before dinner?"

Just then an air horn fired off two short blasts and Papa's eyes lit up like it was the warning shot. That was followed by one long blast. I drew back the curtains and there was Frank, his new Peterbilt parked in the middle of Wood Street. Chrome wheels, chrome bumper, chrome intake and chrome exhaust. All that silver shook the sunlight and the flap on the exhaust danced up and down, breathing puffs of black smoke. Frank gave two more blasts and when I turned around Papa was gone.

I ran through the kitchen and out the back door, glancing up at the peonies and then down the alley, but Papa was nowhere in sight. I snapped a pink peony from the bush and held it to my nose. The fragrance calmed me. I stood there, breathing deeply, slowly, thinking of how Papa called them the healing flowers. "It's because Hercules was healed with the fragrance of a pink peony," he said. But I have never believed his stories about ancient gods.

I was standing like that when Frank crossed the lawn. "Hey, June." He slipped his hand into my back pocket and kissed me on the lips. "Come on," he said, tugging at my jeans. "She's a real beauty." He lifted his new Peterbilt cap off, and snugged it on my head. "I've got something else, too."

"What?" I said. I'd never seen Frank so excited, and I didn't often see him without his cap. He's nearly as bald as a chrome wheel, with tufts of iron-gray hair above his ears. He's only thirty-two but he looks older. I pressed the peony to my cheek and thought about letting my own hair grow, down to my shoulders, to my waist. But Frank asks me to keep it short. I do.

Frank rambled on about contracts and logbooks and fuel costs and tires, but all I wanted to do was call Aunt Helen and asked her to please come take care of Papa. She wouldn't, and I knew that. She wasn't able. And then I could see Papa in some small room at the County Home. I could see him wandering the halls in his blue bathrobe, mumbling details about fogs and frosts.

Frank took the peony from my hand said, "Come on, June. Let's go for a spin."

"Can we drive to the quarry?"

"If you help me wash off the dust when we get back." He winked and tugged the cap down over my ears.

As we stepped into the street the sun poked a hole through the clouds and a circle of light fell onto the truck. The metallic paint glowed. I slid my finger along the pinstriping and, brushing my forearm over the front fender, I said, "It's beautiful, Frank."

"It's our baby," he said.

When I opened the door, Papa said, "I'll bet this baby cost more than a house on Forest Drive."

"Papa," I said. "Get down from there." His hands glided over the wheel and he laughed, tugging on the air horn. "Sweeter than Dizzy Gillespie," he said. He bounced up and down in the seat, a purring sound rolling off his lips. "Coming through," he hollered. He held fast to the horn. "Coming through."

"Glad you like it," Frank said. But Papa didn't move. And then Frank hugged me around the waist and lifted me off the running board. As he stepped up and reached for the handle, Papa slammed the door on his back and hit the horn again. Frank gave a short cry and laid both hands on the base of his spine. "Damn it to hell," he said. "Shut the thing off."

"Stand back," Papa shouted. And the air brakes hissed as the truck lunged and jerked forward. I jumped onto the running board and slid my arm through the handle on the side of the cab. "Stop him," Frank yelled. "For Christ's sake shut that thing down before he kills someone."

I tugged at the door handle, watching Papa trace the shifting pattern on the dash with his finger. We jerked forward and then as I finally managed to open the door and grab the wheel, Papa gave the rig a burst of fuel. My head lashed back against the doorjamb and I screamed, "Papa!" But he just laughed, "Hold on!" I could hear Frank screaming and cussing, and the motion was suddenly smoother, we were beginning to roll, and I glanced back to see Frank, with one hand on his spine and the other raised in the air, and the engine was humming now, and I heard Frank yell, "The brake, the brake, hit the brake," and when Papa pressed in the clutch to shift gears, I threw myself across his lap and snapped on the emergency brake. The engine coughed and shivered like a dying old man, and the truck jolted forward a few more times before we finally stopped. Papa smiled and said, "How'd I do?"

Frank's face was twisted to one side, and as he lifted me down from the cab, he said, "Get the hell out my rig."

That's the first time Frank ever spoke to Papa like that. I could barely extend my arm to help Papa down. He sank into the black vinyl seat, still smiling, and the clusters of instruments seemed to be awaiting his touch.

"Let's take this baby for a drive," Papa said.

Frank pulled out his Redman tobacco and stuffed a few leaves into the side of his mouth. I watched his spit strike the yellow line in the street.

"After dinner," I said.

"We can't eat now," Papa said. "Frank just put in a fresh chew."

"I noticed," I said.

"Go on and eat without me," Frank said. "I've got to make some calls about the trailer."

"Nonsense," Papa said. "It's Sunday. And we've been having Sunday dinners together for years. Ain't that right, Frank?"

Frank spit again, roiled the chew in his mouth, and said, "Yes, that's true all right." He seemed to suddenly relax, as if it would be all right.

"Come on, Frank. Let's take a spin with Papa."

"Maybe around the block," Frank said. He wiped his mouth on his sleeve and his lips peeled back as he worked the chew deeper into his jaw. "Can you get Mr. Peterbilt out of the driver's seat?"

I slapped Papa on the thigh and slid in beside him. We cruised down Center Street, Papa with his arm hanging out the window, his hand banging the side of the door. All the while he's bouncing on the seat, whooping and hollering, but quietly, as if not to bother Frank. We wheeled around the circle twice just so Papa could be certain he'd seen Mr. and Mrs. Wynne on the bench. "Would you look at that?" he said. "They're holding hands."

Then I remembered the potatoes simmering on the stove.

"Head for home, Frank. I left the burner on."

Papa howled as Frank gave her the fuel and we hung a right, whipped down Main Street with Papa yelling about the horn, me fighting to keep his hands off it, and then Frank tapped it for some kid on a bike and Papa managed to grab the cord, and he held it all the way up Mauch Chunk Street. Frank was laughing too, now, and he ran the stop sign at five points, took the turn too wide, cut into Bickert's front yard with the tires, and then Papa let loose with a yodel and Frank slapped his thigh and I just sat there between them, wishing I'd had a cowboy hat and pointed boots.

"That's the way," Papa said. "By golly, boy, now you can drive."

I climbed over Papa and was halfway up the steps when Frank yelled, "Forget cooking. Let's go to Caesar's."

So I snapped off the burner and stuck the potatoes with a fork. Done, I thought. As I wiped my hands, Frank hit the horn a couple times. Or maybe it was Papa. I glanced at the high-oak cupboards. At the tarnished brass knobs, and then at the slate sink. There was Papa's buttermilk glass, dirty, with specks of pepper stuck to the sides of the glass. And the African violet on the windowsill needed water. I paused, heard the horn again, longer this time, and I wanted to stay. I wanted Frank to stay. I slipped the dishtowel through the drawer handle and wiped my cheek on my sleeve.

All the way up Route 512 Papa talked about the frost and how the newsmen had failed to predict it. Frank told him it'd never frost so late in May. Papa said, "What do you know about the weather?" And then Frank said he figured he knew about as much as Papa did and there was no way it would frost on the last day in May. "It's Memorial Day," Frank said, as if this made frost impossible. "It's never frosted on Memorial Day."

"That's what you think," Papa said.

When we pulled into Caesar's I noticed that the wind had stopped. Papa licked his finger, raised his hand, and, after a moment, pointed to the gap in the mountains. "It's trouble," Papa said. "Big trouble."

"So let it frost," Frank said. He rolled his tongue, dropped the chew into the palm of his hand and tossed it under an old Buick. I watched it break apart when it hit. I was beginning to think Papa was right. The sun was still high above the ridge, but the bottoms of the clouds looked as if someone had painted them red. Papa pointed to the north and said, "When's the last time you saw the sun and the moon in the sky at the same time?"

"Yesterday," Frank said.

"See?" Papa said.

Frank slid my hair behind my ear with his finger. I rubbed my shoulder against his arm.

"June knows," Papa said.

"Knows what?" Frank asked.

"How it was in '65."

"Please," I said. "Can we go eat?"

Frank and I sipped coffee and Papa grumbled about the lack of good buttermilk. Frank told him he ought to be glad they even had buttermilk, said Papa was the only man alive who still drank the stuff. I was waiting for them to argue again when Frank reached into his back pocket and handed me a plain white envelope. I thought maybe it was a gift certificate from Horn's Jewelry. Frank had said once that blue jeans and flannel shirts were the only thing he could buy with certainty. I'd told him he did okay with the blue jeans, but the shirts were the awfulest plaids I'd ever seen. I held the envelope to the window.

"What's that?" Papa said.

"Open it," Frank said.

"Is this my surprise?"

"What surprise?" Papa said.

Inside was nothing but a contract from l-D Packing in Des Moines.

"Oh," I said.

"Oh?" Frank said. "Is that all you can say?"

"What's in there?" Papa said.

"Nothing, Papa."

"Nothing?" Frank cried. "Nothing?"

With that, Papa snatched the letter from my hands. Frank reached across the table, knocking over my water glass. Papa said, "Be careful." He smiled at

Frank, holding the letter behind his back. I mopped up the water with a pile of napkins while Frank cussed under his breath, and then the waitress came and asked if everything was all right, and would we like some more water. Papa said, "Sure." Frank said, "Please." I rested my elbows on the table, propped my chin on my knuckles, and sighed. I thought about having both of them sent to the County Home.

We ate without talking. Papa stared out the window at the gap in the mountain. The ham was too salty but the applesauce was fine. It cooled my throat. Papa said the liver and onions were the best he'd ever had and asked if we could come back next Sunday. Frank left two dollars for a tip and I watched Papa to make sure he didn't pocket the bills.

It was dusk by the time we passed Schoeneck Farms. The first cutting of alfalfa was thick and sweet in the air and the moon hung so close to the horizon it looked like someone had stuck it on top of Lone Star's silo. The whiteness shone on the hood of the truck, and through the side-view mirror I watched the mountains disappear into the darkness. Headlights raced up behind us, then dimmed. I wondered how it would be to live my life in this seat, the steady hum of the diesel always in front of me, the lights of the console showing nothing but gauges and numbers. The land always bouncing and twisting away in the mirrors. And how many trips would it take for the tires to wear smooth? For the new smells to wear thin? I looked over at Papa. His head rested on the back of the seat. He was sound asleep.

"We find ways," I said, mostly to myself, wondering if I'd learn how to drive.

"Ways to what?" Frank asked.

I slipped my arm over his shoulder and said, "Wonder how the sleeper will be?"

"Let's try it."

"Not tonight." No, tonight I would talk with Papa. I would call Aunt Helen, get some papers in order. Tomorrow morning Papa and I will carry a bouquet of peonies to the quarry. We'll scatter them on the water. I'll call the County Home.

Frank rested his hand on my thigh and kissed me on the very corner of my lips. It was then that I realized the truck had stopped. We were home. He lifted my left hand, gently placing a ring in my palm, and, holding his hand flat against mine, he kissed me again. I listened to the rattle of the engine, the familiar rise and fall, and I listened to Papa's breathing, and from somewhere I could hear Frank's voice. The sounds had become one, like the whine of a locust in some distant tree. And I could smell the faint odor of fuel and of exhaust, and of men. My chest felt like it was full of limestone dust. "June," Frank whispered. Glancing at him I slid the ring on my finger and spread my hand on the dash. The streetlamp cast a small, almost eerie shadow behind the stone.

Papa said, "It's pretty." His voice startled me, and he said the word pretty again and again until we were in the house and I had to ask him to stop.

Before I could say anything else to him he slipped off to his room and closed the door. I lay on the sofa, covering myself with one of Mama's old quilts. I waited for the weather report, but I fell asleep. It was after two when I woke to the sound of Papa's voice. He was singing, yodeling. When I leaned my head against the banister the sound grew fainter, and in its place I heard a hammering. I went to the kitchen, pulled back the curtains, and there, in the back yard, in his pajamas and robe, was Papa. He was driving stakes around the peony bushes, singing in a low, quiet voice, almost humming.

He moved with a determined slowness, and I must have watched him for nearly an hour. When he finished driving the stakes he draped blankets over them, covering the bushes so that the frost would not fall on the blossoms. He pulled a single blossom from the red-hearted bush and sat on the lawn.

I pressed my cheek to the glass and listened as he started his song again, and then yodeled. I huddled closer to the window, and when his voice grew so silent that I could hear nothing but my own breathing, I pulled the quilt tight around my shoulders and drew the curtains. Those flowers, I thought. Those flowers. And I tried to finish the thought, to say that Papa's life was not my life. But for all its truth, all I could say was those flowers. Those flowers and that man.

Blueline 9 (1988)

School's Out

Scott LeGow had graduated third out of his class of thirty-one at Silver Lake High School, a mathematical ratio he often conjured when he was thinking about where he stood in the world. Number one and two, of course had been girls. It wasn't so bad for a boy to be third. None of the guys thought you were too much of a grind or a sissy, as long as they didn't know your highest grades had been English and Social Studies, straight A's since eighth grade. And the amazing fact was you had come within a *single decimal point* of having to give a speech in front of everybody in town, so you said a prayer of thanks for that C in Personal Hygiene fall semester—not that you had come to class dirty, but you had refused to talk about the consequences of living in a filthy house.

When Scott heard Kyla Bradley and Debby Serrano give their nearly identical sorry-to-leave-my-hometown speeches, blurted out as if they were rushing to finish a phone call before the operator asked them to deposit another quarter—when he heard their meaningless philosophizing, he was glad it was them and not him up there. His topic might have been, "I'm glad to leave this town," supported by detailed evidence. And people would have wondered six months later why he hadn't. People always knew who had gone away and who hadn't usually and usually why. Byron St. Pierre had gone off to RPI to study engineering. Kyla had enrolled at Potsdam State for music; Debby at Cornell for home economics.

After the top three, you had the rest of the top ten listed on the program in order of rank—including the only other boy, Byron St. Pierre, six foot six and totally uncoordinated, who would have ranked higher except he had flunked gym every year since eighth grade. Scott would have been happier if the other boy in the top ten had been "normal." Of course if he had been the only boy it would have been a lot worse.

The top ten boys and girls sat on stage with the principal and the school board, while the other students were out on the gymnasium floor with the families. Everybody figured the bottom twenty-one were better off unranked on the program, though most everybody knew thirty and thirty-one had to be Wanda Shink and Kevin Shink, who were second cousins or fourth cousins depending on how you figured it, and there had been strong competition from the four other Shinks in the class. But even Wanda and Kevin got awards, although Kevin hadn't been there to pick his up, and there was considerable doubt as to whether he had really graduated.

Old Wanda, who must have been twenty, already had one baby and was showing even in her maroon gown from her next pregnancy, heaved herself on stage and picked up her citizenship award. There was an interesting restriction on that award, though it had not been spelled out in the program. A kindly doctor, summer resident of the Town of Lost River for many years but now deceased, had endowed an award for the descendants of the three original families who had settled the township, a citizenship award that was supposed to encourage the children from these families, all very poor now, to live a better life. The three families were Benson, Luke, and Shink. There were still plenty of Shinks around, but the other two families had more or less merged with the Shinks, who continued to merge with each other to produce future candidates for the award. Some years the award was not given (although there might very well be a Shink graduating), since the doctor had stipulated that no juvenile delinquent was eligible. The previous year there had been a record eight Shinks on the roster at Silver Lake High School, but the award wasn't given, because all eight had DWI convictions, one had an aggravated assault, and another was already serving time at Dannemora for armed robbery. Wanda Shink had never been in that kind of trouble, so she was the proud recipient of the Dr. Orris Weedon Citizenship Award for 1979—two hundred dollars, a hundred more than any other award given at graduation. "To buy Pampers and baby food," a woman's voice said out loud in a neutral tone, speaking for everybody there. No one said, "Shh." And no one laughed.

Scott received no money for his efforts. He had to settle for two certificates in black vinyl folders and a bronze sports trophy—but maybe his efforts *had* paid off, indirectly. Somebody important had noticed him. Diane Olmstead had been seated on stage as a school board member. She'd given a brief speech about the generosity of the Town and its leading citizens, and assisted in handing out the diplomas. After the program she'd gone over to Scott and introduced herself, as if it were the first time they had ever spoken, or the fact of the cap and gown made him a stranger to her. She'd hired him on the spot, five dollars an hour with possible bonuses. "We need a reliable young man to help Kenny in the shop, and you're the one. Everyone in town is quite impressed with your achievement." Just like that, as Scott had no say in the decision.

He had wondered if it was just another version of the Dr. Weedon Award, a pity award. He wondered if Diane had looked around to see whether his notorious father had dragged himself out of the house for the ceremony—or allowed his mother to go—and noticing nobody from LeGow's, felt sorry for Scott and decided to give him an award he didn't really deserve.

"I'm not a mechanic," he said. "I got a B in shop this year, you know." He assumed his grades were part of the public record.

"That doesn't matter. Kenny just wants somebody he can train. A good intelligent young man. You have to be intelligent to have gotten this far."

"I'm not very intelligent. I almost flunked math."

"No you didn't."

No use lying to her. She knew all of his grades.

Try another reason: "But I don't have a car and I don't even think I can get rides."

"And *I* have an answer to any reason you can come up with," she said, straightening his cap and fiddling with the tassel. "Free room and board. Your own cabin. You don't even need a car."

"Okay. I'll ask my parents."

"You're eighteen. You don't need to do that anymore."

She spoke as if she knew him before, and he remembered the day clearly.

He was ten years old and his grandfather was up on the mountain where he was the fire tower observer. The old dark green Chrysler with a state decal was parked by itself at the gravel turnoff where the brown sign said, TRAIL TO HOGBACK MOUNTAIN FIRE TOWER, ELEVATION 2510 FEET, STATE OF NEW YORK CONSERVATION DEPARTMENT, FIRE TOWER OPEN, and high school kids had painted their names on the boulder to the right of the trailhead. Scott used to try and match the names to the faces he knew. It was a Tuesday and Buckskin was supposed to have come down off mountain on Monday morning to get supplies at the store and take a bath or at least jump in the lake. Buckskin had a log cabin across the Cedar Lake highway from LeGow's, but some years later the state took over the property, tore down the cabin, and Scott remembered seeing the logs spread out by the side of the highway waiting to be hauled away. The remains of Buckskin's cabin made him think of toy logs, lying around after somebody played with them.

The day Buckskin didn't come down was the day Scott had first spoken to Diane, although he had bought candy at the old store when he was much younger, pushing nickels and pennies across the Formica counter without looking up at the face that told him "thank you for the exact change" and "come back soon" every time, a politeness that made him smile because it was so strange.

The day his grandfather had failed to come down off the mountain, Scott's mother told him to get on his bike and go look for his father. He didn't ask her why she didn't just pick up the phone and call the most likely places where his father might be found; even then, he knew what his mother hated to do. But he didn't know why she asked her boys to do it for her. Either Greg or Scott—they'd both become old hands at finding what bar their father had chosen to conduct the day's business. He could have chosen the Balsam, the Pinnacle, the Eagles' Nest; or when he'd gotten adventurous, the Lost River Inn, or even the Timberline out where the power line ended and the real wilderness began. Never the same bar, because the people who owned them wouldn't put up with Jack LeGow two times in a row. They'd walk him out to his car and tell him, "Drive home carefully and don't come back soon." Nowadays Jack LeGow never went out. The LeGows had home delivery from North Country Liquor.

You could almost track him down by seeing which way the tree branches bent, or how the waves on Silver Lake crisscrossed in an odd wind—if you believed, as Scott did at the time, that Jack LeGow could unsettle nature by his mere existence. You could follow the skid marks on the highway, the oil spots that dripped from his car engine every twenty feet it seemed. To find his father, Scott might have to ride ten miles to Timberline—the last place he'd look—but his bike was used to the ups and downs and he rode without much effort, standing on the pedals sometimes near the top of a hill when he ran out of momentum. Often he'd dawdle along the way, shoot down the hill toward a stream he knew about, the sort of minor waterfall you'd never hear from a car even with the windows rolled down. He could spend a whole afternoon at a secret place like that. He had no wristwatch, and all he had to go by was the one o'clock siren down at the firehouse and the sound of Klingman's bread truck rumbling down to the valley, usually at three.

The time Buckskin didn't come down from Hogback Mountain, Scott took no side trips. After checking the bar at the Eagles' Nest, where they hooted at him and said "You're a year late, kid" and worse things—he rode his bike across the South Kilns meadow into the hamlet of North Bay, past the boat shop that had tried to repossess his father's Evinrude and the side road that used to be the old state highway, where he didn't like to ride his bike because the people never tied up their rabid dogs. There were all kinds of side roads Scott had only tried once, roads that quickly became ungraded dirt jeep trails spiraling up the hollow until they were steeper than a mountain trail, with Shinks living in various cantilevered tar paper shanties and mobile homes and buses with no mailbox.

Lost River Inn sat right out along the highway in plain view. Scott could see his father's '69 Valiant snuggled up to the front porch as if the car felt more at home there than any other place in the world, and that the three other cars parked there didn't have as much claim to that comfort. The Christmas lights strung along the eaves of the porch made Scott feel as though it was all right for him to be there, kids were welcome and Santa Claus might even drop by in the middle of summer. There weren't any green or blue lights, just red and yellow, so he wondered whether they were really Christmas lights.

Otherwise, the Lost River Inn was not very welcoming. It smelled of creosote and old batteries and the rotten sofa on the porch where according to local rumor a man had lain dead three days without anybody noticing or doing anything about it. Another version was that Scott's father had lain there the same amount of time, almost dead. And stank like a dead man. The two-story building was basically covered with green tar paper, one end of which was blowing loose in the wind, and the white shutters were closed on all six upstairs windows. He wondered whether anybody lived up there. A sign on the porch said ROOMS BY THE MONTH. Inside, all the bars he knew were basically the same.

So it was not as though Scott opened the door without the slightest idea what he would find inside. Straight ahead was the bar itself, with the deer antlers hanging from the varnished beam, more Christmas lights, this time blue and green, strung around the beam and then wrapped a couple of times around the antlers to keep them from falling on somebody's head. He saw the Genesee beer sign with snow-capped mountains that could not have existed in the Adirondacks that he knew; nor the picture of a giant shark-like fish lunging out of an old illustrated map of Silver Lake, where nobody had caught anything over five pounds during Scott's life; and the photo that was tacked to the lower right-hand corner of the map must have been taken in the fifties, Fred the bartender was a very young man holding up the record catch for the decade.

A dollar bill tempted Scott from its fake gold picture frame, as did the beef sticks in a tall jar, just out of reach. He hadn't eaten lunch.

His father seemed to be sleeping at his bar stool, arms forming a nest for his head, his red and green checked flannel shirt untucked from his olive green pants, as if someone had come by and said, "Your shirt's on fire. Now it's out." Kids did that at school. School was out.

"Dad."

No answer. No sound except a radio somewhere buzzing halfway between two stations.

Scott tapped him on the back. "Dad?"

"One more for the road," his father mumbled. But there was no bartender in sight. Footsteps overhead made the water stained ceiling creak like a sick bird singing. Another customer, one of the heavier Shinks, dressed in size sixty bib overalls, was propped against the wall and seemed to be chuckling about a private joke.

"Dad, Mom wants you."

His father moved his head. "Did somebody say something? Who's that? Hey, Fred, there's a little kid in the bar. Little kid pissing on the floor." There was a puddle of beer near his father's stool, or something that looked like beer. "Who's in charge here tonight?"

Actually, it was the middle of the afternoon, but you couldn't tell from inside the bar. Scott's father sat up, swiveled on the stool and squinted as if there were a tremendous gust of light coming from the doorway, but the door was closed and the bar was almost dark, with a blue glow from the Christmas lights the only major source of illumination.

"Dad, Mom wants you." Very quietly, hoping to get it over with soon, not really caring, after all, whether his father could understand what he told him. He would say it once more, then ride home on his bike and report that he had tried to get his father's attention. He heard a woman clear her throat. She sat in a booth along the front, and Scott could see the top of her head.

His father pinched his shoulder. "Hey little squirt! What are you doing out of school?" Finally, he had recognized him and maybe figured out what time of the day it was, but his father never spoke Scott's name to him. He must have felt that speaking his son's name would have given him the impression that he cared and had feelings. "Your mother tell you you didn't have to go to school today?"

"Dad, it's July." In an even tone, hoping not to get a reaction. "School's out, Dad."

Scott's father looked at his wrist, where there wasn't even the tanned outline of a wristwatch. "How did you get here? She out there now? Afraid to come in? Well, screw her!"

"I rode my bike. Mom's looking for Buckskin. She wants your help."

"Mom's looking for Buckskin." His father imitated him in a prissy tone. "Well, he ain't here. So quit your whining, go home and eat supper." He tucked his shirt in and smiled like he was suppressing a belch. "Anybody here seen an old man trying to look like a cowboy and Indian? The famous Wild Bill Hickok and Tonto all in one." No answer. "Maybe she oughta check the Eagles' Nest. Ain't that where the old fart goes when he comes off the mountain? Goes right upstairs looking for Trudy Benson?" Scott's father was directing his questions towards anyone who might know the answer, certainly not towards Scott.

The overweight Shink in the corner cleared his throat and said, "Trudy's been dead ten years, Jack. You, of all people, ought to know that." Chuckled again, thumbs hooked around the straps of his overalls.

"Shut up, Wendell."

"I don't make up the facts. I just report 'em."

"Then how much do you weigh now, Wendell? What's the latest report?" No answer. "Well, that'll shut you up."

"Dad?" His father seemed to have forgotten he was there.

"You have to *yell* like that? You want me to punch you in the mouth to make you shut up? What the hell are you doing here on a school day?" Scott shrugged his shoulders. "They'll whip you senseless over at school when they find out where you been hanging out." He looked around the bar, smiling, as if the other three customers would back him up on this promise.

The lady stood up in the booth. She was just a silhouette against the blue light and cigarette smoke. "Jack, is this your boy?" she said.

"Who the hell are you?"

"Open your eyes. You know me."

"Trudy?"

"Jack, you know who I am. Is this Scott?" Back then people were always asking who he was, because he looked so much like his brother. Sometimes they'd ask, "Is this Greg?" At least one asked the right question. Scott's father stood up and tried to walk towards the woman, but staggered and grabbed at the next bar stool. It was like he had slipped on ice.

"I need another. Where the hell is Fred?"

The lady came up to Scott and touched his shoulder. She was taller than his mother. "Scott, I'll take you home right now." And that was the first time he ever really looked at Diane, riding home in her new pickup listening to the tape deck play acid rock, his bike tied down in the back and covered with a tarp, because it would rain so hard they would have to pull off at the side of the road, and Diane kept the radio going while they waited. Turned down the volume when she wanted to tell him something. "That's a shame when someone forgets the seasons," she said. "That comes from staying inside too long, a terrible thing to do even on a rainy day. Your father used to know the difference between a rain storm and an ice storm, but now, well, I hate to think about how he's changed. Your father knew when school was in session, when it wasn't. He wasn't a bad student either, after all. Nor was Wendell, in his day. He's the smart one in that family. But he hasn't been outdoors for twenty years."

Scott hardly knew Diane then, and he looked at her with wonder as she tapped the steering wheel and sang along with the tape. Listening to her sing, he forgot for a moment why he had been riding around from bar to bar on his bike. Years later, when he was out of school for good, he would go through the scene again, blow up every detail as if he were studying a complicated photograph.

Wendell Shink. He lived above the bar, in one of the rooms Fred rented out. The year Wendell graduated from high school—what year would that have been? 1950? Wendell's father might have grabbed him by the front of the shirt and said, "It's all rot, what you learned in school, fat boy. Now go and live your life the way you were born to live it, as the town drunk. It isn't a bad life after all. The hours are good. Actually, you set your own hours, none of this getting up for school the same time every morning with a goddamn buzzer going every ten minutes. School's out, boy. Join the real world." Wendell still lived in that room above the bar. Scott knew which one. Most nights it was the only light on the second floor, when you drove by your own way to a better place. But you knew Wendell was up there in his room doing whatever he did as part of his routine. He might have had a TV up there.

Wendell might have come close to having to give a speech at one point in his life. At the beginning of the school year, he sat at his desk, if he had one, composing the speech, "What I'll miss the most when I leave Lost River." He wrote a fine speech, listing the natural beauty of the town, the closeness of the community. He read it over, looking for mistakes, errors in fact. He got scared. When school was out, he wondered whether he might leave Lost River; but he never did, and he told the people at the bar who would listen that when the time came, they'd have to carry him out and he knew that would get a good laugh.

Blueline 10 (1989)

Sea Change

Although she sat reclined against the windshield with her back to him, Guy could imagine her as minutely as if she faced him—the green crescent moons of her sunglasses obscuring the green, shimmery full moons of her eyes. After nearly twelve years of marriage, her eyes still troubled him, their evanescent character, changeable and indecipherable like the rippling form of some object dropped overboard, a Danforth anchor, a rubber glove, glimpsed beneath three feet of incoming tide. Likely, an iridescent jag of fish scales streaked her jaw like war paint where she'd scratched at a mosquito bite or rubbed at some salt film with her gloved fingertip. She did not like fishing bare-handed. The fishy smell, the cold, eely feel of the fish unsettled her. He could envision what others, even on the closest inspection, would overlook: the faintest tan line on the fair-skinned backs of her thighs where her white canvas shorts hitched up when she fished leaning out over the bow. More a line of light freckles, really, on the otherwise white thighs, barely rounded and firm as fish bellies. An almost imperceptible modulation. Guy wondered if her lover, Dewey, had noticed it.

Maisie turned her head to him against the wind. "There," she yelled and pointed the still scurfy finger of her glove.

Guy could not hear her over the racing motor, but he knew what she wanted. She preferred trawling in the small coves around Whaleboat, near the ledges where he had to watch for rocks ravenous for a good bite of hull. She liked to idle or drift in a coming tide, a flexible pole responsive to a tugging current in hand. He had reservations about her sportsmanship, but he conceded that she had the knack, the luck or the instinct to select the right fishing grounds and a natural jigging style that magically out-fished anyone else aboard.

"Here." She turned her head again. "I've got a good feeling about this spot."

He cut the motor, but not before she dropped her jig over with the boat still underway. He'd warned her about fouling the propeller, but she ignored him, as she always did, grinning. He shook his head. With an economy of energy he admired, she flicked the hook from the cork handle with her thumbnail, dropped it, untwirling the line as she experimented with the length by flicking her wrist. She liked to set the hook just about an inch below where the sun last glinted off it, the very depth at which she could not spot the fish, but the fish could spot the sparkling lure. Maisie believed that you could not catch the fish you saw, only the ones you could not see.

She rose from the starboard seat and plopped down on the bow, setting her feet wide apart, facing him now. His eyes ran up the thighs, never tan in the summer, just that darker shade of pale, to the dark, kelp-like hair of her crotch, a shadow glimpsed deep in the bell of her shorts' leg. Had Dewey ever met her in the summer when, complaining of the heat, Maisie would strip off layers of clothing by degrees as if they corresponded to the shrinking red thread of the mercury? Had she surprised Dewey some logy July afternoon in a stuffy motel room stripping off her shorts, her tank top with only her skin between him and his desire? Guy adjusted the line on a fender.

"Do you think you will catch anything?" he asked.

She smirked. "Only someone who hates fishing would ask that. Fishing isn't a means or an end."

"I know," Guy said. "Fishing is a participle not a noun. Process, process."

She laughed with him, the first laugh they had shared since he had discovered the letters. He had not been looking for them, as Maisie had accused him. He felt as if they had been looking for him, this packet of letters, well-thumbed, dated, but out of order, neatly tied with a pink ribbon, as if they were curious about what sort of husband could miss such obvious evidence of a protracted affair. He had merely been looking for Maisie's social security number for a tax form when the letters confronted him. He had not read them.

Maisie smiled at him, sun glinting off her glasses. She completed their well-rehearsed repartee, "Fishing, Guy, is very Zen," then lowered her eyes to the water's surface, which, glimmering blue sky and sun, revealed nothing. What, Guy wondered, did she see with her intent, lens-blinkered eyes?

She sat, focused, but not still. Her jigging involved a snap and relax. Neither completely action nor stillness, her sport was all attention—movement and not movement. Her eyes fixed on the water, all the intensity concentrated in the whip of her wrist, willing the fish to her hook. Guy would be taxed to say whether she was an extension of the pole or it of her until that last jerk when the monofilament tightened, the line stretched between her hunger and the mackerel's, her life, its death, and, in a single arc, her arm bowed and the fish soared onto the deck in a rainbow of spray and speckle of scales and squirmed, pinned beneath her tennis shoe as she bent to disengage the hook from its agape mouth.

Guy hated her then, coolly, as coolly as she tossed the fish aft for him to clean with his buck knife on the cutting board while she resumed her perch on the bow. She averted her eyes from the stern and his end of the operation.

"How many is that?" she asked.

"Sixteen," he answered. "Sixteen mackerel and one pogy."

"Pogies don't count," she said.

"Only to other pogies." Guy patted his jeans pockets for his knife.

"Only to sixteen," Maisie said and laughed.

Guy didn't laugh. Fishing should be more of a sport than a tally sheet, he thought. He dropped the mackerel into the joint compound bucket that doubled as "the head" in moments of undeniable need. He fished around in the locker for the cutting board, opened the buck knife, removed the fish and lopped off its head and tail. He slit it along the backbone in the new method their eighty-year-old island neighbor, Avery, had taught him. "Less blood than when you slice the stomach," Avery said, "and the backbone lifts out neatly." It was true; the backbone did yield easily.

Sitting in the sun, grilling in the oily fish and motor odors, Guy drooped, spineless and oozy himself, as he melded with the sticky vinyl of the seat. Why didn't he ever tell her, "Stop. Enough. Stop fishing?" She wouldn't clean the mackerel. She rarely even ate them. She enjoyed mackerel fishing because she didn't have to mash live bait on the hook. She protected herself from the squiggly, wormy, cold feel of death. She wore gloves. She refused to learn how to operate the boat. She hailed him as if she were a deb hiring some taxi hacker to take her out for a night at the operetta. For Maisie, fishing was all allure, all attraction. But she was good at it. Sometimes she threw fish back.

"Strike," she called, then added, "only another pogy." She tossed the fish astern. "You can throw it over if you like."

He didn't like. He flipped the filleted mackerel into the bucket and washed his hands over the side of the boat. He scanned for rocks, then shook his hands dry. The boat gleamed with a residue of fish slime, pearled like butterfly wings or a sequined, palatine floor in Oz. Gorgeous but insubstantial. Illusory. He dipped a sponge over the side and scrubbed the floor around the gas tanks, succeeding only in smearing the shimmery slick over himself, the sponge, the tanks.

The pogy flopped acrobatically, trying to backflip over the gunnels. Guy thought of salmon ladders, flying fish. Biology urges the impossible even for pogies. Pauhaugen, the Algonguians used them and named them for fertilizer. Bluefish anglers used pogies for bait. Food fish for soil and fish. Living sacrifices. Guy felt suddenly sorry for the fish. He scooped it up, but, before he could toss it over, it caught his eye with its own. Lidless, cold, and completely devoid of anything he could name—panic, desire—its eye rimmed nothing. Pure instinct. A life of reflex.

"Garbage fish," he said and tossed it over. The pogy vanished before it split the water. Protective coloration.

"Literally garbage," Maisie called in agreement.

This summer the pogies had schooled so thick that they'd suffocated themselves, de-oxygenated the water. The bodies had washed to shore where they were rotting in piles that even the indiscriminative gulls wouldn't touch. The stench polluted the coast and rivaled the weather in conversational popularity. The local favorite saw was: the only good to come of this stink is that, by contrast, the tourists don't smell so bad.

Walking down to the outhaul, he and Maisie had had to crunch and slip their way over shingles of decaying menhaden. "Dead Pogies' Society," Maisie had punned. He had laughed. But Avery didn't find the phenomenon funny.

"Never seen it this bad—not in eighty years," he'd commented to Guy the previous evening. "Oh, I've seen it happen before, of course, but never thick as this. Pshew." Avery had shaken his head. "It's like something right out of Revelations. A plague. Unnatural."

But Guy didn't think it was apocalyptic, just a smelly turn of the life cycle.

"Hey, your fishwife's got another," Maisie yelled. She threw her pole down and hauled in on the line with her gloved hands. The line slipped. She tromped down on the line with her left sneaker and peeled off her right glove with her teeth. Her sunglasses plopped into the water. She kept the line tight and yelled, "It's a derby fish for sure. Moby mackerel." And then the fish sliced out of the water. Maisie trapped him neatly beneath her foot. "Look at him, Guy. Just look at him."

But he couldn't. He was looking at her, her teeth and lips smeared with mackerel phosphorus, grinning, her hair, almost white now with its black streaks snaking through, salt-frizzed, her long triumphant arm hoisting the fish by the tail as if she were counterweighing it, and her eyes, darting, by turns, blue and green, restless as a dragonfly. He had never loved her more. She had never appeared more beautiful. Wanting her, he could not blame any man for wanting her. And, for a moment, he wished to tell her that, to tell her she was forgiven. But she had already returned to her fishing, unsnarling the line, muttering about the ten dollar pair of sunglasses she wouldn't be able to replace until the next mainland trip. So instead he said, "He's a keeper."

"You bet," she called back without looking up at him. "What do you think of the old lady now?"

"Holy mackerel," he said. And they shared a second laugh. He sat down to clean the monster. "Think I'll find Jonah inside?" he asked. But the wind carried the question away from her. She didn't respond. He checked the water for rocks, but here, on the lee side, they were drifting away from the ledges. Maisie would want to motor in closer soon.

As he chopped the head off the mackerel, it shuddered in protest, and the shudder vibrated sympathetically up his own spine. He slit along the spine, spread the sides like wings and slapped out the stomach. Some brit, entire, spilled out. Once he'd found a jig among the brit, swallowed whole.

As he worked, he wondered at his sudden impulse to shout his forgiveness to Maisie. She had never asked for forgiveness. She did not believe she'd sinned. No sin, no remorse. And, after the initial shock of the discovery, he realized that he didn't believe she had sinned either. He did not need to forgive her adultery. In truth, he thought monogamy overrated. When he'd asked Maisie "Why?" she'd responded, "Why not?" He'd been stumped for an answer. They had no children with delicate psyches to damage. They'd never explicitly agreed that marriage implied monogamy. He'd acted on that assumption; she had not. But it was, he acknowledged, his assumption. Their sex life had attained a middle age of uninspired, monthly regularity, as predictable as a full moon or Maisie's menses, natural and unsurprising. So why had he felt this urge to forgive her? To forgive her for what?

He scraped the offal from the cutting board with the edge of the blade and watched it sink into the water. He hoped Maisie wouldn't catch him; she thought the gore scared off other fish. He didn't think fish thought deeply enough to make the connection. Usually the chum attracted gulls whose squawking alerted Maisie to his misdeed. But today the sea-pigeons lacked interest.

Privately, he thought of tossing the innards overboard as a sacrifice—a blood sacrament to feed other fish so they would multiply, plentify the seas. But, thinking that, the image he'd suppressed all week surfaced. The dead pogies hadn't disturbed him; the live ones had.

A humpback whale had driven a school of pogies into the cove off Orrs. A local fisherman had seined the cove in, hoping to tempt the humpback with a free lunch into an extended visit.

Maisie had coaxed Guy to make the day trip to Orrs. "The whale will take our minds off us for awhile," she'd argued. They'd packed a picnic and motored over. The whale had awed Maisie. Guy had been too busy navigating away from the nets and other whale watchers to ogle. He'd finally secured the painter to one of the floats on the net. But the surfacing whale had not impressed him. Neither had the spume from the blowhole. What had impressed him, and impressed him morbidly, was the view down. The water surface stretched deceptively placid, but some slight movement had distracted him, and he'd glanced down into the water at the teeming, turbulent churning of innumerable pogies. Unable to exit the cove, they reeled and eeled in a fishy mass, fathomless, futile. The vision dizzied him with a midnight vertigo, a chthonic nightmare bellied up into daylit scrutiny.

As the memory repossessed him, he understood his impulse to forgive. How had Maisie for five years lived this other life, this other love, and obscured it from him? Was the Maisie Dewey knew the same Maisie who had fried mackerel for him, the same one whose dreams mumbled at his night after night? Was Dewey's Maisie his wife who told bad puns and had an almost imperceptible tan line on the backs of her thighs? Or did Dewey love some other Maisie, some woman unknowable to him?

He had not read Dewey's letters; he did not know if this man, this name, this ink on paper, loved her at all. He did not feel as if Dewey had robbed him. Maisie's body belonged to her alone. But who lived inside it? What swam and gasped and schooled in her, refusing to surface? The certainty that he knew her had been ripped from him, gashed a hole in his life and filled it with this strange presence, this creature yanked from its element and flopping on the wide deck of their bed. Strange to him, alive and cold. A semblance of Maisie but disemboweled. Trophy fish. He shivered. The sun had slipped. The tide had shifted. He sensed the change in the drag of the boat and sluice of the water.

He dropped the filleted mackerel into the bucket and stared at Maisie. What could he say to her? She'd already promised to cut Dewey free—no phone calls, no letters, no contact. She'd burned the letters, returned all mementos. But he could not force her to unremember him. He had had to sacrifice his memory of her, his understanding of her. But she had not had to sacrifice, or, if she had, he could not confirm it. He could not break her surface to verify anything, and he found himself wishing some mild violence on her, a nick of the jig in her perfect calf, a sneakery slip, a bruised shin. Something to break the surface, just ding it a little. But she sat beyond the reach of his ill will.

"Call it a day?" he asked. But even as he posed the suggestion, he watched the pole bend like a bow.

"Another sea monster," Maisie cried, snapping to her feet, but, just as suddenly, the line twanged. The unmet fish shot like an arrow through black water. She pursed her lips in the briefest disappointment, then chattered excitedly, "A dogfish. I'm sure of it, Guy. I could tell by the feel of it. Avery said they're teethy. Snap. They strike just like that."

"You probably just snagged a pot warp," Guy said. But he knew it was untrue. No buoys nearby. He just couldn't bear her excitement.

"Well." She slapped her palms against her hips. "No hook. No fish. Call it a day?" She spiraled the fluttering line around the pole.

He turned the key. The motor thrummed. Over the noise, he hadn't heard her approaching. She surprised him, her salty, fishy, lips plumping against his.

He held her tight, so tight that she couldn't squirm out of his arms. She turned her face into the hollow of his neck and mumbled, "It was a great day, Guy, a great day for mackerel fishing."

He thought of the dogfish jetting off with the souvenir jig hooking into its stomach. Fish were lucky; they had no memories. Maisie raised her head and kissed his cheek, surprising him again. She still had the power to surprise him, and, Guy realized, that power arose from her unknowability. And he thought how the flip side of the traits we most hated in others were those we most loved.

Maisie nestled into the cabin seat across from him. "It's gotten cooler," she said. She wriggled into her sweatshirt and drew her knees up inside it. "I think I'll sit in here instead of the bow." The slap of the hull on the waves, the motor's drone suspended conversation until Maisie, looking up at him, yelled, hands cupping her mouth, "I'm sorry. I'm sorry about the hurt to you," an apology which would elsewhere be a whisper. He reached his left hand and stroked her wind-snarled hair.

"Maisie," he said. And he felt something tug free, or rather he felt himself set something free—a pogie, an eely qualm about this woman he loved, perhaps even a jealousy he would not admit to himself—plenty of fish in the sea. He grinned at her and removed his hand, returned it to the hard round of the helm. The spray struck the sun with prisms. The boat bounced crest to crest. Crossing the bay with Maisie, he forgave her so completely that he would not remember to tell her so for many years.

Blueline 22 (2001)

Pond

Michael stood by the pond in an early mist, allowing the quiet coolness and his presence in it to bring to him stealthy, imprecise images of generations of men standing by wooded ponds at dawn to ponder their wishes and hopes, images of men seeking meaning in the water, the trees, and the beginnings of day. Though he considered himself ill-suited for such musings—he was simply a man by a pond at daybreak—he liked the feel of secrecy around the pond. Angela and her parents were still asleep in the house up the hill, and as he walked he allowed himself a sense of childlike hiding and aloneness; as if no one else had ever been in this place, and knowledge of his secret was kept, quiet and dark, somewhere at the bottom of the water.

But the pond, where later in the day they might all gather for a picnic, was no secret place. It was the pride of his father-in-law's land. Andrew himself visited it on many mornings at dawn and he, Michael knew, did indeed come to consider his place in the world. He used the pond analogically in discussing everything from the baseball pennant races to American foreign policy. He reminded his daughter of her childhood discoveries along its shore. He would point out that this pond was in shape and spirit much like Thoreau's. His concept of the seasons was defined by the changes he saw in the life of the pond, from the appearance of the first bloom of the water lilies to the patterns formed by ice-locked maple leaves.

Andrew's intensity made Michael's early visit more real, more secret. Around the pond with Angela and her parents he was offhand and indifferent, adopting an attitude of deflator to the older man's reverential statements. "It's a pond," he would say to Andrew, waving a careless hand in the air. "It's got fish and weeds and water, just like any other little water body." And Andrew would tell him that he was mistaken—that the pond not only held the biological treasures to which Michael so casually referred, but also the history and caring of a family that had looked over it now for four generations. Their debates were endless and benign, retaining a mootness which each respected. It was only alone in the dawn that Michael could summon even his tenuous images of communion with the world, and these were unspecific, almost as though he satisfied a role assigned by the setting.

At breakfast Angela was withdrawn, nearly sullen. She did not like to awaken and find Michael out of bed. At home and everywhere else, she was the first up. It was she, on a Saturday morning, who would come back into their bedroom at eight-thirty to ask if he intended to sleep away any more of one of the limited number of Saturdays still left in his life. He would then stay in bed a little longer. As with his father-in-law and the pond, he was edged, in the Saturday morning ritual, into a role he was not sure he sought; he found himself a willing foil for someone else's more fervid feelings.

The breakfast—perfectly tan toast, bacon, and tightly scrambled eggs, black-flecked with pepper and bacon grease—was delicious to Michael. Maria appreciated a good breakfast as much as he did. Over her daughter's protests about ruining a morning with all the time it took to prepare such greasy, unhealthy food, Maria cooked hot, full breakfasts each day of their visit. Angela drank coffee. When Michael and Angela were alone at the table, with only her newspaper separating them across the table, he asked her what she planned to do with her day.

"Something foolish," she said immediately.

He laughed easily, aware that she had reached some midpoint in her irritation with him. In her comment was a signal that she had left any real anger behind, if indeed there had been any, and had entered the transition of mild joking. It was within the context of gentle self-mockery that they reoffered themselves after they had disagreed.

"What foolish?"

"I'll think of something," she said. "I may take a nap."

Again he laughed. Naps were as foreign to her as late sleeping.

"I'm not kidding," she said, moving the newspaper away from her face. "I may take a nap. Or drive into town and buy myself four or five greasy burgers. To catch up with the rest of you."

"Are we picnicking by the water this afternoon?" he said.

"Of course. Unless I take off."

It was the mark of their yearly summer visits to her parents that after four or five days of the stay Angela became what she could only later characterize as "slightly testy." Across from her at the dining room table Michael felt sure that she had now reached that state, having glided easily into it from her mild pique over his beating her out of bed. In a week or two, at home, she would blame it on the cooler climate and her mother's old-fashioned, oil-laden cooking. Then, within another two or three weeks she would blame it on herself and sit down to write her parents a long, girlish letter to apologize and to say how much she looked forward to the next visit. Michael's vision of his wife's pattern of behavior during and after the visit was clear, but not to be shared. Mention of it during its unfolding was as useless as warning a child that he is becoming tired. But knowledge of the cycle allowed Michael a moment of tender, private love for the girl who had grown up here and married him, eight years ago, at the edge of the pond he had visited earlier.

Shortly after noon Maria began massing ingredients for the picnic. Containers of all sizes and all covered in some way or another with aluminum foil were placed on the kitchen table. She dispatched the men to carry the picnic table down the hill. When they returned Maria was moving easily around her kitchen, pausing with a forefinger at her lips and speaking an occasional food word. When she had filled the table she directed the other three in the chore of delivery. She assigned Michael on his first trip down a big, platter-shaped expanse of aluminum foil. "Cut up vegetables," she said. "Don't slosh it around too much."

On his way down the hill Michael was aware that during his first few visits to this house he had felt himself an intruder into the picnics, an odd fourth. Then, largely through Maria's almost solicitous attitude toward him—making him carry the biggest platters, sending him back up the hill for things forgotten, preparing his favorite foods—he had come to feel himself a part of the picnic. By now their meals by the pond were a known ritual, from the discussions the day before to the debates over placement of the table and Andrew's frequent comments about some aspect of the pond and its history.

Sitting around the table in the warmth of a summer day, they enjoyed Maria's raw vegetables, the tiny meat sandwiches, and her potato and macaroni salads. There was no breeze at all, and beside them the pond, except where broken by plant life, was smooth and glassy. The meal was quiet, toned perhaps by Angela's not-unfriendly distance. Michael sought his wife's eyes several times in their silence. After her mid-morning flirtation with recovery, she had relapsed into quiet. Now she ate slowly, as if in thought. Michael was tempted to be irritated with her.

Maria stood, as if made uncomfortable by the weight of the stillness around them. "What shall I get more of?" she said, too brightly.

"I could use some more tea," Andrew said, taking another carrot.

Angela stood from the table and, without words, took the tea pitcher from her mother and started up the hill toward the house. The other three sat in silence until she had disappeared.

"Never has outgrown her moods, has she, Michael?" Andrew said.

"No, I suppose not," Michael said, surprised at Andrew's comment.

"She used to get like that for several days at a time when she was a girl," Andrew said. "Not unfriendly, just silent."

"She was just growing up," Maria said.

"Oh yes," Andrew said, "but she has brought her moods along."

As he helped himself to what was surely his fifth or sixth little sandwich, Michael realized that Angela was taking a long time to refill the tea pitcher. His glanced moved from the house to her parents, who were looking too. It was as if the three of them, even with food, conversation, and the pond, were not fully at ease without Angela there.

"I'll go see if she needs some help," Maria said, standing.

Again her trip up the hill was stopped by her daughter. Angela carried no tea, and was dressed in a gray, one-piece bathing suit. Maria remained standing for a moment, and then looked toward the men.

"What's this?" Andrew said to Michael. "She gave up on that suit when she was in high school. She hasn't grown much, has she?"

Angela came down the hill slowly, her hair loose at her shoulders and her arms swinging in the warm air. The suit fit her perfectly. In style it was modest, covering her thoroughly from below her shoulders to the top of her legs. But at the same time, with its blockish construction and tight fit, it was as appealing as anything Michael had ever seen on her. Her small breasts were carried softly against the worn gray fabric. The points of her pelvic bone were nearly arrogant in their definition. The young woman in the girl's gray suit struck Michael as a beautiful addition to the afternoon.

She walked by the table, picking up a celery stick as she went, and headed toward the pond. Her mother sat down. Angela approached the pond, and as she did her father stood, as if by reflex. "Angela, what are you doing?" he said, a hand at his forehead.

Angela did not answer him, but squatted to splash at the water.

"Angela," her father said, and took several steps in her direction, "you're not going in the pond? Nobody has ever gone in the pond to swim." He spoke with a slightly incredulous tone and moved with the same attitude in his limbs, as though he were approaching a wild animal in the woods. Still Angela said nothing.

Having tested the water with her hand, she stood and brushed at the hair on her neck, as she did when she pulled it from beneath the collar of a coat she had just put on. She extended her arms upward, stretching the thin body in the perfect gray suit, and dove into the water.

"Maria?" Andrew said, walking toward the table with open palms.

"I thought she'd be up by now," Maria said. "I didn't know it was so deep."

"Oh, I suppose it's almost ten feet out there in the middle," Andrew said, looking alternately at Maria and the pond. "But what is she doing? She knows it's a looking pond."

After what seemed to be nearly a minute, Angela emerged at the far side of the pond and stood up. She pulled hair and weeds from her face and then disappeared again with a light, smooth dive.

"What is she doing?" her father asked anyone. His attitude, free of anger, was made of blank wonder. "She'll scare the fish to death and rip up all the plant life." He waved a hand in the air.

Again Angela was gone for what seemed too long a time. Michael sat easily at the table, picturing the strong, fluid strokes of his wife under the water. Andrew continued his bewildered glances here and there. He looked at the water as if it had suddenly turned red, or disappeared. When Angela appeared again on the near bank, he moved quickly toward her.

"What are you doing?" he said with forced patience. "Angela, it's a looking pond. It's for the plants and the fish, and for us to look at." He might have used the same tone of voice with a small child who was seeing the pond for the first time.

Angela stood still near the edge of the water. She held herself in the manner of a little girl who had just passed her first swimming test. And to Michael at least, she appeared at the same time to be a perfect, coy mermaid sent up to them from a secret spot at the bottom of the pond. With the sunlight dancing in the water droplets on her face she seemed ready to laugh—to be answering to some piece of girlhood which had awakened inside her.

"Angela," Andrew said, continuing his fatherly tone, "people in this family have been looking at this pond for nearly a hundred years. Your own great uncle wrote beautiful poems out here. You and I have spent hours down here, talking and learning."

Angela pushed her hair back with both hands and smiled. "Oh, but I've discovered something that no one else has ever been allowed to know," she said. "It's wet." She laughed and stepped closer to her father, as if to show him her wetness. She looked up into his face with an exaggerated smile and began walking the two of them back to the table, a wet arm around his shoulders. She guided him to his seat and then stood behind him with her hands draped over his collarbones, as though assuring herself that he would remain seated. From behind her father she ventured shy smiles at her husband and her mother, and then sat down next to Andrew, whose face still carried shifting looks of wonder. Michael built himself another small sandwich. Maria stood, as if to consider the tea once more, and then sat down. Andrew slowly wedged a carrot stick into his thoughts. Angela shivered once despite the warmth, and beside them the pond, glassy and thick, had erased all traces of the aberrant swimmer.

Blueline 5 (1984)

CONTRIBUTORS

June Frankland Baker, originally from Schenectady County, graduated from State University of New York at Albany and taught in North Syracuse and Skaneateles, New York, and Longmont, Colorado. She lives now in Richland, Washington. Her poems have appeared in numerous literary journals and anthologies. June is married and has two daughters.

Linda Batt freelances to national magazines from her farm in DeKalb, New York. Her articles appear in *The Writer; Country; Rural Heritage; Fur, Fish, and Game; Mothering;* and other publications. She is a frequent contributor to *Blueline.*

Laurie J. Bergamini's work has appeared in literary journals such as *Dark Horse, The Windless Orchard,* and *North Country.* She lives in Lake Placid, New York.

Elizabeth Biller-Chapman was born in Boston, graduated from Smith College, and took a Ph.D. from Columbia in 1969. Formerly a teacher of Renaissance literature and a psychotherapist, she now lives and writes in Palo Alto, California, with her husband, new kitten, and lovely garden. In 1995 her chapbook, *Creekwater,* won the (M)other Tongue Press international competition. Bellowing Ark Press in Shoreline, Washington, published her first full-length collection, *First Orchard,* in June 1999. Her poems have appeared in *Yankee, Poet Lore, Prairie Schooner,* and *Poetry.*

Jonathan Blake teaches at Worcester State College in the Languages and Literature Department. His work has appeared in *Poetry East, Two Rivers Review,* and *Worcester Magazine,* among others.

Joseph Bruchac lives with his wife, Carol, in the Adirondack foothills town of Greenfield Center, New York, where he was raised. Much of his writing draws on that region and his Abenaki ancestry—part of an ethnic background that includes Slovak and English blood. He, his younger sister, Margaret, and his two grown sons, James and Jesse,

239

have worked extensively to preserve Abenaki language and culture. An internationally known storyteller, he has been featured at the National Storytelling Festival in Jonesborough, Tennessee, and the British Storytelling Festival. His honors include a Rockefeller humanities fellowship, an NEA poetry fellowship, the Wordcraft Circle Storyteller of the Year Award, and the Lifetime Achievement Award from the Native Writers Circle of the Americas. His poems, articles, and stories have appeared in more than five hundred publications, from *National Geographic* to *American Poetry Review,* and he has edited such highly praised anthologies as *Songs from This Earth on Turtle's Back* and *Returning the Gift.* His more than one hundred books range from children's literature to fiction, poetry, and nonfiction for adult readers. Recent titles include *Sacajawea,* a novel, *Crazy Horse's Visions,* a picture book, and his autobiography, *Bowman's Store.*

Neal Burdick is a North Country native and Phi Beta Kappa graduate of St. Lawrence University. He has been a summer theater technician; a high school English, drama, and outdoor ed. teacher in Maine; a railroad worker in New Hampshire; and a wilderness survival instructor in the Adirondacks. He lives in Canton, New York, where he is a publications writer/editor and an advanced writing instructor at St. Lawrence University, and codirector of its Young Writers Conference. As a freelance editor and writer, he has published poetry, short fiction, reviews, essays, introductions, chapters, and articles in local, regional, and national magazines and newspapers, and edited many books for regional publishers. He is editor of *Adirondac,* the award-winning magazine of the Adirondack Mountain Club, and of the club's series of hiking guides and other publications, and a frequent contributor to *Adirondack Explorer* and *Adirondack Life.* He has been a juror for the New York Foundation for the Arts creative nonfiction grants program, and for "The Writing Contest," cosponsored by North Country Public Radio and the Adirondack Center for Writing, on whose steering committee he serves. He is the coeditor of *Living North Country: Essays on Life and Landscapes in Northern New York* (North Country Books, 2001) and in 1999 was a panelist on regional writing at the Associated Writing Programs national meeting.

David Chura grew up in upstate New York and now lives in Connecticut. He has taught at-risk adolescents for the past twenty-five years. His essays and poems have appeared in such publications as the *New York Times, The Anthology of New England Writers, Turning Wheel, English Journal,* and *Essential Love: A Poetry Anthology.*

Jeffrey Clapp's poems and stories have appeared in many journals. He has just finished "Don Juan in New Hampshire," a book-length narrative poem, and is at work on a sequel. He is a professor of English at Dutchess Community College in Poughkeepsie, New York.

Arthur L. Clements, poet and critic, teaches at Binghamton University. He has been granted fellowships by the SUNY Research Foundation, the Virginia Center for the Creative Arts, and the National Endowment for the Humanities. His poetry has received a John Donne Award, the Dylan Thomas Award, the Allen Ginsberg Award, and a Poetry Center Award, among other honors. He has also received both the Chancellor's Award and the University Award for Excellence in Teaching. His scholarly publications include *The Mystical Poetry of Thomas Traherne* (Harvard Univ. Press), *Poetry of Contemplation* (SUNY Press), and a second edition of *John Donne's Poetry* (Norton). His books of poems include *The Book of Madness and Love* (Bordighera), *Dream of Flying* (Endless Mountains), and *Common Blessings* (Lincoln Springs), which received the American Literary Translators Association Award for translation into Italian and publication in a bilingual edition, *Benedizioni Comuni* (Cross-Cultural Communications). He recently completed *Five Hundred Years of Italian-American Accomplishments* and is currently at work on a book of memoirs and on another book of poetry.

Helen Collins was born in 1905 in New York City. She grew up in Troy, New York, and attended Russell Sage College. In 1931 she married an RPI student, John Collins of Blue Mountain Lake. She was a secretary at the Troy Conservatory of Music and he was an engineer. They both lost their jobs to the Depression and moved to Blue Mountain to help John's parents run their hotel business, The Hedges, working with her extended family and raising her own. In 1982, she took a writing course with *Blueline*'s founding editor, Alice Gilborn, and became one of the first contributing writers to the magazine.

Susan Comninos graduated from Cornell University in 1989. Her work has appeared in a number of journals, including *houses in motion* and *Cornfield Review.*

Joan Connor is an assistant professor in fiction writing at Ohio University. She has published two collections of short stories: *Here on Old Route 7*, and *We Who Live Apart.* Recent work has appeared in the *Ohio Review, Southern Review, The Journal, Arts and Letters, TriQuarterly, Gettysburg Review, Kenyon Review,* and *Manoa.* A recipient of an Ohio State Arts Council grant, she lives in Athens, Ohio, and in Belmont, Vermont, with her son, Kerry.

Paul Corrigan lives in Greenville, Maine, on the shores of Moosehead Lake. He has published two books of poetry. His poems have appeared in *Yankee, Beloit Poetry Journal,* and *Poetry Northwest.* He has taught in poetry-in-the-schools programs and in high school English classes. He and his wife enjoy traveling, reading, and numerous outdoor activities.

Tony Cosier, of Nepean, Ontario, a retired high school teacher who now writes full time, is widely published in magazines and anthologies internationally. The author of eight volumes of poetry, three plays, and *Ensemble,* a book of short stories, his most recent collection is *Clearwater Tarn* (Penumbra Press).

Stephanie Coyne-DeGhett is a poet and an instructor in the Department of English and Communication at SUNY Potsdam, where she teaches primarily in the writing program. Her love of words and place have found expression in her position as poetry editor for *Blueline*. Her work has been published widely.

Pamela Lee Cranston was born in New York City and was raised in Old Deerfield, Massachusetts. She and her family have had close association with the High Peaks region of the Adirondacks for over fifty years. She received her B.A. from San Francisco State University in 1984 and in 1988 received a Masters of Divinity degree from the Church Divinity School of the Pacific. Ordained an Episcopal priest in 1990, she has served San Francisco Bay area churches and hospices for the past fourteen years. Her books include *The Madonna Murders* (Dry Bones Press), *Clery Wellness and Mutual Ministry,* and *An Eccentric English Journey* (privately published). Her poetry, essays, and book reviews have been published in numerous journals including the *Adirondack Review, Anglican Theological Review, On the Trail: An Outdoor Anthology, EarthLight, Journal of Christianity and Literature, Mystic River Review,* and *Women: Empowering and Healing.* She lives with her husband in Oakland, California, and returns to the Adirondacks regularly.

Peter Cummings teaches English and comparative literature, with a focus on Shakespeare, at Hobart and William Smith Colleges in Geneva, New York. He has been returning to the Adirondacks for over thirty years, in all seasons, and has now returned to the sonnet form, writing over four hundred of them on a recent sabbatical leave.

Annie Dawid teaches at Lewis and Clark College in Portland, Oregon. *York Ferry,* a novel, was published by Cane Hill Press. Her recent collection of stories, *Lily in the Desert,* was published by Carnegie Mellon University Press in 2001.

Marcia Derouchia lives in a wooded area outside Potsdam, New York, and is employed by Clarkson University.

Bob Dial currently works as an information specialist for InfoEd in Guilderland, New York. He has previously worked as a television listings editor, landscaper, and daily newspaper reporter. He is a graduate of the State University of New York at Cortland and lives with his wife, Joanne, in Glenville, New York.

Linda Dyer lives in Amherst, New Hampshire. Her work has appeared in *Slant, Birmingham Poetry Review, Heartbeat of New England,* and other journals and anthologies as well as in newspapers, including the *Christian Science Monitor* and the *New York Times.* In 2001, she was awarded first prize in creative nonfiction by the online journal *Poet's Canvas.* She is currently working on a book, *Willa Cather in Jaffrey: Portrait of a Writer at Work.*

Sherry Fairchok earned her M.F.A. in poetry from Sarah Lawrence College in 1997. Her chapbook "A Stone That Burns" won the Ledge 1999 Chapbook Prize. Her full-length manuscript *What They Wanted Me to Bring Back* was a finalist for the Agnes Lynch Starrett Prize sponsored by Pittsburgh University Press. Her poetry has appeared in the *Southern Review, Ploughshares, DoubleTake*, and other journals.

Sean T. Finn earned his B.A. from Vassar College and has spent much of his life traveling, painting, and writing novels, short stories, and poetry. He recently spent six months living in a Zen monastery in upstate New York.

Allen C. Fischer, a former director of marketing for a large corporation, splits his time between Saugerties and Brooklyn, New York. He has had poems published in *Atlanta Review, Poetry, Prairie Schooner,* and *River Styx.*

Jim Flosdorf is a professor emeritus of Russell Sage College of the Sage Colleges, where he taught English literature and creative writing. He has published two books of poetry, *Temagami* and *Rivertown.* He is also the author of *My Father Was Shiva,* a biography/autobiography in poetry and prose. He is one of the founding members of the Hudson Valley Writers Guild.

CB Follett's poems have appeared in magazines and anthologies worldwide. She has been a five-time nominee for the Pushcart Prize in Poetry, a runner-up for the Robert Winner Prize and the George Bogin Award, and a finalist for the Alice Fay Di Castagnola Award. She has received contest honors in the Billee Murray Denny, New Letters Prize, the Anne Stanford Prize, and the Glimmer Train Poetry Contest, as well as a grant from the Marin Arts Council. She has published four poetry collections: *The Latitudes of Their Going* (Hot Pepper Press, 1993), *Gathering the Mountains* (Hot Pepper Press, 1995), *Visible Bones* (Plain View Press, 1998), and *At the Turning of the Light* (Salmon Run Press, 2001), winner of the National Poetry Book Award. Her latest anthology, for which she was editor, is GRRRRR: *A Collection of Poems About* BEARS (Arctos Press, 1999). With Susan Terris, she has started a new poetry annual, *Runes: A Review of Poetry.* She is also a painter and sculptor and has done illustrations and covers for GRRRRR, *Visible Bones,* and *At the Turning of the Light.* A graduate of Smith College, she lives with her husband in Sausalito, California.

Walt Franklin notes that "one year" of living in an Appalachian hollow of western New York has suddenly become twenty years of having fun and keeping a low profile.

Pam French earned a B.A. from Hollins College before working as a reader for Doubleday and as a "mammal keeper" for the New York Zoological Society. *Misty Hill Press,*

Yankee, Long Island Quarterly Review, Angleflesh Press, Wood Thrush Press, and *Potomac Review* have all recently published her poetry.

Myra Gann, a critic of drama and poetry and a translator from the Spanish, became involved with *Blueline* in 1988, while she was a professor of Spanish in the Department of Modern Languages at SUNY Potsdam. Over the next five years, she served on the magazine in several editorial capacities, including fiction editor, art editor, and layout editor. She is now retired from both the university and the magazine.

Eric Gansworth (Onondaga), visiting associate professor of English at Canisius College in Buffalo, New York, was born and raised on the Tuscarora Indian Reservation in western New York. A novel, *Indian Summers,* and a book of poems and paintings, *Nickel Eclipse: Iroquois Moon,* have been published by Michigan State University Press. His work—poetry, fiction, and visual art—has been in numerous anthologies and journals. Additionally, his paintings and photographs have appeared in a number of exhibits in New York State, including the Herd about Buffalo public arts project. He serves on the Board of Directors for Hallwalls Contemporary Art Center, has served on the literature panel for the New York State Council on the Arts, and is currently on the Artists Advisory Committee of the New York Foundation for the Arts. He recently completed a second novel.

Alice Wolf Gilborn is the founding editor of *Blueline* and a former editor of books and publications at the Adirondack Museum in Blue Mountain Lake, New York. She now lives with her husband, Craig, in Mt. Tabor, Vermont.

Albert Glover was born in 1942 in Boston, Massachusetts, and grew up in the nearby town of Needham. He graduated from McGill University in 1964 (first honors in English and the Peterson Prize for poetry) and received a Ph.D. from the State University of New York at Buffalo in 1968 where he studied with Charles Olson, Robert Duncan, Robert Creeley, and other poets associated with the Black Mountain School. An edited form of his dissertation, *Charles Olson: Letters for Origin,* was published by Jonathan Cape in 1970 and reprinted by Paragon House in 1988. In 1968 Glover joined the English department at St. Lawrence University in Canton, New York, where he is currently Anne and Frank P. Piskor Professor of English. He regularly teaches courses in poetry writing, modern British and American poetry, and contemporary American poetry. He has published four book-length collections of poetry: *A Trio in G* (Frontier Press, 1971), NEXT (Burn Books, 1981), *The Dinner Guest and Other Poems* (Glover Publishing, 1990), and RELAX YR FACE (Glover Publishing, 1998), as well as several chapbooks including *The Mushroom* (IFS, 1972), *Paradise Valley* (Bellevue Press, 1975), and *Songs and Sonnets* (Rootdrinker, 1986). He is also editor and publisher of *River of Dreams: American Poems from the St. Lawrence River Valley,* and, for the Institute of Further Studies, the collaborative epic *A Curriculum of the Soul,* a project in process since 1971.

Daniel Green started writing poetry at age eighty-two. He has published over one thousand poems in over two hundred fifty magazines and journals. He has three collections: *Late Start* (1989), *On Second Thought* (1992), and *Better Late* (1995).

John Grey is an Australian-born poet, playwright, and musician. His work has been published in *South Carolina Review, Poet Lore, Passages North,* and *National Forum.* He won the 1998 Rhysling Award for Science Fiction Poetry.

Lois Marie Harrod's sixth book of poetry, *Spelling the World Backward* (2000), was published by Palanquin Press, which also published her chapbook *This Is a Story You Already Know* (1999) and her book *Part of the Deeper Sea* (1997). Her poems have appeared in many journals, among them *American Poetry Review, Carolina Quarterly, Southern Poetry Review, American Pen, Prairie Schooner, Literary Review, Zone Three,* and *Green Mountain Review.* Her earlier publications include the books *Every Twinge a Verdict* (Belle Mead Press, 1987), *Crazy Alice* (Belle Mead Press, 1991), and a chapbook *Green Snake Riding* (New Spirit Press, 1994). She received 1993 and 1998 fellowships from the New Jersey Council of the Arts for her poetry. She is the supervisor of creative writing at the New Jersey Governor's School of the Arts, and teaches English at Voorhees High School in Glen Gardner, New Jersey.

Joanne Hayhurst lives in the Berkshire hills of northwest Connecticut. Over the past few years, she has had a number of poems published in periodicals including *Blueline.* One poem, published by *Prairie Schooner,* was nominated for the 2002 Pushcart Prize. Her work was analyzed in *By Herself: Women Reclaim Poetry,* edited by Molly McQuade (2000), and presented in *Fruitflesh: Seeds of Inspiration for Women Who Write,* by Gayle Brandeis (2001). Pending acceptance of her book-length manuscript, "What Daphne Said," she was awarded the M.F.A. in poetry from Warren Wilson College.

Dianna Henning was awarded a California Arts Council residency for their artist-in-residence program 2001–2002. She has taught creative writing in several California prisons and directed the Arts in Corrections program in Susanville, California. She holds an M.F.A. in writing from Vermont College (1989). She won Eastern Washington University's fellowship to the Writer's Center in Dublin, Ireland, in the summer of 1994. Her work has appeared in *The Sacramento Anthology: One Hundred Poems, Fugue, Red Rock Review, Peregrine, Spoon River Poetry Review, Crazyhorse,* and the *Mid-American Poetry Review,* among others. She has won several awards for her fiction.

Rick Henry is an associate professor and the director of graduate studies in the Department of English and Communication at SUNY Potsdam. In addition to his book *Pretending and Meaning: Toward a Pragmatic Theory of Fictional Discourse* (1996) and articles on pragmatics and parody, he has published fiction in a variety of journals. He took over from Anthony O. Tyler as the editor of *Blueline* in 1998.

Allen Hoey's manuscript *A Fire in the Cold House of Being* was selected by Galway Kinnell for the 1985 Camden Poetry Prize; the collection was published by the Walt Whitman Center in 1987. His second collection, *What Persists,* was published in 1992. Poems and essays have appeared in *American Poetry Review, Georgia Review, Hudson Review,* and *Southern Review,* among others. He is the 2001 Bucks County poet laureate, recipient of a Pennsylvania Council on the Arts fellowship, and a teacher of writing, literature, and Buddhism at Bucks County Community College.

Robert Hunter's poetry has appeared in many magazines, including *Cresset, Indefinite Space, Pittsburgh Post-Gazette* and others. He lives in Manchester, Vermont.

M. J. Iuppa lives on a small farm near the shores of Lake Ontario. Most recent poems have appeared in *Poetry, Tar River Poetry, Comstock Review, Buckle and Mockingbird, Eclipse, Haz Mat Review, Coffee House, Into the Teeth of the Wind,* and *Yankee.* Her creative nonfiction is included in *In Brief: Short Takes on the Personal,* edited by Judith Kitchen and Mary Paumier Jones (Norton, 1999), and in *Chelsea.* Her chapbooks are *Sometimes Simply* (Forseeable Future Press, 1996) and *Temptations* (Foothills Publishing, 2001). She is writer-in-residence at St. John Fisher College and curates the Genessee Reading Series at Writers and Books in Rochester, New York.

Maurice Kenny was born in Watertown, New York, and has taught at the State University of New York at Potsdam, the University of Oklahoma, and North Community College. He is the author of more than fifteen books including *Between Two Rivers, Wounds Beneath the Flesh,* and *Tekonwatonti/Molly Brant (1735–1795): Poems of War* (poetry); *Rain and Other Fictions* and *Tortured Skins and Other Fictions* (fiction); and *Backward to Forward: Prose Pieces* (essays).

Betsy Kepes lives a stone's throw north of the blueline in Pierrepont, New York. She is a music teacher, freelance writer, and amateur historian. Each summer she lives in a little glass house with her family on top of Coolwater Ridge in northern Idaho where she is a forest fire lookout.

Ann B. Knox's collection of short fiction, *Late Summer Break,* was published by Papier Mache Press. She has two prize-winning books of poetry, *Stonecrop* and *Staying Is Nowhere.* She has been visiting the Adirondacks for seventy-five years.

Norbert Krapf, a native of southern Indiana, has directed the C. W. Post Poetry Center of Long Island University since 1985. His poetry collections include *Somewhere in South-*

ern Indiana, Bittersweet Along the Expressway, and *The Country I Come From.* He received the Lucille Medwick Memorial Award from the Poetry Society of America.

J. L. Kubicek is a retired social worker, World War II infantry veteran, bibliophile, and gardener.

Sue Ellen Kuzma is a singer and voice teacher. Her poetry has appeared in *Sahara, Diner, Ekphrasis, Issue,* and *American Journal of Nursing.* She resides in Natick, Massachusetts, and is on the faculty of Trinity Rep Conservatory in Providence. She is at work on a manuscript entitled "This Jonquil-Toned Joy."

Margaret Lamb has twice taken sabbaticals from her legal career to work as an air taxi pilot.

Gina Larkin was a teacher of religion in a large Catholic high school for many years. She is now retired and writes full time.

Burgess Lawrence lives and writes in the North Country, which suits his interest in the beauty of the natural world. He has published in *Snowy Egret,* as well as written feature articles about living in the North Country of upstate New York.

Marcia Lawther is an editor of *In Style* magazine in New York City. Her poems have appeared in *Ladies, Start Your Engines* (Faber and Faber), *Caliban, Margin, Harvard Advocate, Wesleyan Younger Poets, Rolling Stone,* and other journals. She has been a finalist for the *Nation,* the 92nd Street Y poetry competition, a *New Letters* Literary Award, and a New York State Arts grant.

Randy Lewis has been writing poetry for years and currently writes a weekly mountain culture column, "Actively Adirondack," in the *Adirondack Daily Enterprise,* the only daily newspaper in the Adirondack Mountains. She is the copy editor for that newspaper and writes for Minnesota Public Radio's *Writer's Almanac.* Other poetry she has written has been published in *Mud Creek* and *Many Moons.*

Lyn Lifshin's most recent prizewinning book (Paterson Poetry Award) is *Before It's Light* (Black Sparrow Press, 1999–2000). *Cold Comfort* was published by Black Sparrow Press (1997, rpt. 2001). They also published *Blue Sheets* in 2002. She has published more than one hundred books of poetry, including *Marilyn Monroe* and *Blue Tattoo,* has won awards for her nonfiction, and has edited four anthologies of women's writing, including *Ariadne's Thread* and *Lips Unsealed.* Her poems have appeared in most literary and poetry magazines and she is the subject of an award-winning documentary film, *Lyn Lifshin:*

Not Made of Glass. Her poem "No More Apologizing" has been called "among the most impressive documents of the women's poetry movement."

Richard Londraville is noted for his publications on Yeats, Pound, and Joyce. His books include *Too Long a Sacrifice: The Letters of Maud Gonne and John Quinn, "Dear Yeats," "Dear Pound," "Dear Ford": Jeanne Robert Foster and Her Circle of Friends,* and *John Quinn: Selected Irish Writers from His Library.* His poetry has been published in many journals and in books, such as *River of Dreams, The Theater Audition Book,* and *Poetry: An Introduction through Writing.* Londraville is a professor emeritus of literature at the State University of New York at Potsdam.

Marjorie Maddox has received numerous awards and fellowships, among them the Paumanok Poetry Award from SUNY-Farmingdale, an Academy of American Poets Prize, a Virginia Center for the Creative Arts Fellowship, and two Pushcart Prize nominations. Her first book, *Perpendicular As I,* won the Sandstone Publishing National Poetry Competition. She has published four chapbooks: *Nightrider to Edinburgh (Amelia,* winner of the 1986 Charles William Duke Long Poem Award), *How to Fit God into a Poem (Painted Bride* 1993 Chapbook Winner), *Ecclesia* (Franciscan University Press, 1997), and *Body Parts* (Anamnesis Press, 1999). She studied with A. R. Ammons, Robert Morgan, Phyllis Janowitz, and Ken McClane at Cornell, where she received the Sage Graduate Fellowship for her M.F.A. in poetry in 1989. She has published over two hundred and fifty poems in such journals as *College English, Poetry, Prairie Schooner,* and *American Literary Review.* Her fiction has appeared in the *Sonora Review* and *Great Stream Review.* Maddox is a professor of literature and writing at Lock Haven University.

Jennifer Magnani was born in Saratoga, New York, and currently lives in Westchester County. She has completed a short story collection, "Minerva Tales," and has published in numerous journals including *Buffalo Spree* and *Footwork.*

Anne Mausolff, after years of teaching and "librarianshipping," retired to Vermont where she hikes, skis, paints, and practices calligraphy.

Arthur McMaster is a poet and playwright and has been published in Ireland and extensively in the United States. His two-act dramatic stage play *Prisms* was produced by Florida Stageworks in 2001.

Richard E. McMullen has published over three hundred poems and three books. He is a World War II and Korean War veteran and has taught English, journalism, and creative writing in Michigan.

Roger Mitchell is the author of seven books of poetry, most recently *The Word for Everything* (1996), *Braid* (1997), and *Savage Baggage* (2001). Awards for his poetry include the Midland Poetry Award, a Borestone Mountain Award, two from the Arvon Foundation, one from P.E.N. International, another from the Chester H. Jones Foundation, plus fellowships from the Indiana Arts Commission and the National Endowment for the Arts. He has also written a work of nonfiction, *Clear Pond: The Reconstruction of a Life*, which won the John Ben Snow Award at Syracuse University Press. He divides his time between Jay, New York, and Bloomington, Indiana.

Michele Mitchell-Weal has studied poetry with Susan Wheeler, David Lehman, and Robert Polito in the New School M.F.A. program in creative writing and with David Trinidad, Phillis Levin, and Rachel Wetzsteon. She's turned many 1986–87 journal entries documenting a paranoid schizophrenic episode into poems, some of which have been published by literary magazines such as *Santa Monica Review* and *Dream International Quarterly*. She is currently working on the 1986–87 journal, turning it into a book composed of entries in different genres called *Acting Up in Therapy*.

Ann Mohin is the author of *The Farm She Was* (Bridge Works, 1998), a *New York Times* notable book. She lives with her husband on a farm in upstate New York where she is currently working on another novel.

Gwen Monohan is a former teacher currently working with the elderly in Virginia. She has published her poetry in *Hard Row to Hoe, Poetry Motel,* and *American Poets and Poetry.* In addition, she has won a Dover Beach Poetry Press Award for her poem "Robin's Wake" and a Windmore Writer's Audience Choice Award for her poem "Simple Machines."

Robert Morgan is a native of North Carolina and has taught at Cornell since 1971. He is the author of the best-selling novel *Gap Creek,* which won the Southern Book Critics Circle Award for Fiction for 2000. In addition to *This Rock* and five other books of fiction, he has published ten volumes of poetry, most recently *Topsoil Road* (LSU Press, 2000).

Howard Nelson has lived in the Finger Lakes and has taught at Cayuga Community College for the past thirty years. His poems appear in four collections, most recently *Bone Music* (Nightshade Press), and various anthologies. He recently edited *Earth, My Likeness*, a selection of Walt Whitman's nature poems, published by Wood Thrush Books.

John Nizalowski was born and raised near Berkshire, New York. He holds a B.A. in English and history from Binghamton University and an M.A. in English from the University of Delaware. He now lives with his daughters Ursula and Isadora in Grand

Junction, Colorado, where he teaches creative writing and composition at Mesa State College and is an associate editor for *Pinyon Magazine*. His work has appeared in *Albany Review, Weber Studies, Bloomsbury Review, Snowy Egret, Harp, Fish Drum, Listening Eye,* and elsewhere.

Peter Obourn lives in Fairport and near Old Forge, New York. He has written poetry and short stories about the Adirondacks and is working on a novel set in the southern tier of New York State.

Kate O'Connell grew up in Saratoga Springs and draws upon her Saratoga experience for her work. Something in a particular place or moment, or a slant of light, will catch her eye and she will begin to write. "Autumn Elms" grew out of such a moment. She recalls seeing the silhouette of graceful elms, dark against the background of a spectacular golden sunset, and the poem began to form itself. She considers her poems to be images evoking emotional responses that tap into a universal reference that is common to just about everyone. For the past eight or nine years, she has been focusing her creative energy on photography.

Katharine O'Flynn spends summers in the Adirondacks. Her work has appeared in *Harpweaver, Storyteller Magazine,* and others.

Adrian Oktenberg has two collections of poetry: *The Bosnia Elegies* (Paris Park Press, 1997) and *Swimming with Dolphins* (Bucknell Univ. Press, 2002). She has won the Astraea Lesbian Writer's Award, the *Americas Review* poetry prize, and the Philip Roth Residency at Bucknell University. She lives in Northampton, Massachusetts.

Eric Ormsby is a long-time contributor to *Blueline*. His poems and essays also appear regularly in such journals as the *New Yorker, New Criterion, Parnassus,* and the *Paris Review*. His poems have been anthologized in the *Norton Anthology of Poetry* and *Norton Introduction to Literature*. In 1997, Grove Press collected his new and selected poems as *For a Modest God*. His fourth and most recent collection, entitled *Araby*, appeared in 2001 with Signal Editions in Montreal. He lives in Montreal and teaches Islamic Studies at McGill University.

Darby Penney's poems have appeared in *Negative Capability, Exquisite Corpse, Thirteenth Moon,* and other journals. She is publisher of the Snail's Pace Press, a literary small press that she edits with her husband, the poet Ken Denberg. Darby earns her living as director of historical projects for the New York State Office of Mental Health. She lives in Cambridge, New York.

Allan Peterson's work has been published widely in magazines such as the *Gettysburg Review, Marlboro Review, Shenandoah, Pleiads, Bellingham Review, Agni, Black Warrior Review,* and *The Journal.* He has two chapbooks: *Small Charities,* #7 (Panhandler Press Chapbook Series) and *Stars on a Wire* (Parallel Editions). He has received fellowships in poetry from the NEA and the state of Florida and has been nominated four times for Pushcart Prizes. He is also a visual artists, chair of the visual arts department at Pensacola Junior College, Florida, and the director of the Switzer Center for Visual Arts.

Carol Potter won the 2000 Balcones Poetry Award and the 1999 CSU Poetry Center Prize for her book of poems, *Short History of Pets.* She has published her poetry in *Poetry, Field, Women's Review of Books, Yankee Magazine,* and *The Pushcart Prize XXVI: Best of the Small Presses.* Her previous two books, both from Alice James Books, are *Before We Were Born* and *Upside Down in the Dark.* Potter lives in western Massachusetts, but much of her time is spent on Brandreth Lake.

Samuel Elias Pritchard is a storyteller from Nazareth, Pennsylvania.

John Radigan is a year-round resident of the Adirondack Park, and has been on the faculty of Paul Smith's College for seventeen years. He holds a Ph.D. in English from Syracuse University and an M.F.A. in poetry from Vermont College. Over the last ten years, he has given numerous readings of his work throughout the North Country, and in 1996 he was awarded an honorable mention in the North Country Writers Festival Contest for a poem in the voice of the famous hermit Noah John Rondeau. His poems have appeared in *Blueline* on several occasions and in a privately printed mini-anthology entitled *Many Moons.* He was also a frequent contributor of poetry book reviews to the literary magazine *Contact/II* before it ceased publication. In addition to writing, his interests include the visual arts, playing the bagpipe, and the philosophy of Albert Schweitzer.

Kurt Rheinheimer's fiction has appeared in many magazines, ranging from *Redbook* and *Playgirl* to *Michigan Quarterly Review* and *Carolina Quarterly.* Stories have been anthologized in four volumes, including *New Stories from the South: The Year's Best* (Algonquin Books). He lives in Roanoke, Virginia, where he is editor of *Blue Ridge Country,* a glossy regional magazine. He and his wife, Gail, live with a varying number of their five sons.

Claudia Ricci, of Spencertown, New York, is a full-time faculty member at the State University of New York at Albany and a former staff member of the *Wall Street Journal.* She has published fiction and poetry in several literary magazines, including *Another Chicago Magazine, Alaska Quarterly, MacGuffin, The Little Magazine, Reed, Thirteenth Moon,*

Yemassee, and *Barkeater.* Her publishing company, Star Root Press, released its first book, *on that day,* in 2001. She published her novel *Dreaming Maples* through the press in 2002. She is the author of three other novels: *Sister Mysteries, Eyes on Orion,* and *Pearly Everlasting.*

Laura Rodley has published in *Massachusetts Review, Juggler's World, Sahara, Sanctuary, Aurorean, Nurturing,* and *Rural Heritage.* She assisted Thurston Munson in completing his mural, "The Green Fields," and donated a painting, "Indian Maidens Maple Sugaring," to the town of Greenfield. It hangs in the Greenfield Town Hall.

Bertha Rogers' poems appear in journals and anthologies and in several collections. Her translation of *Beowulf* was published by Birch Brook Press in 2000. She has won residency fellowships to MacDowell and other U.S. artists' colonies and to the Hawthornden International Writers Retreat (Scotland) and the Julia and David White Artists Colony (Costa Rica). She was a feature poet at the International Poetry Festival in Quebec in 2001. In 1992 she founded Bright Hill Press/Word Thursdays, a nonprofit New York State literary organization.

Liz Rosenberg is the author of three books of poetry, two novels, and numerous books for young readers, including four prize-winning poetry anthologies. She lives with her husband, son, and dogs in Binghamton, New York, where she teaches at the State University of New York at Binghamton.

John Rothfork is in the English Department at Northern Arizona University where he develops and teaches online courses for an M.A. program in professional and technical writing. He has had three Fulbright scholarships to Asia and has edited the *New Mexico Humanities Review* for fifteen years. His latest poetry book, *Donny Does Email,* was serially published by Amarillo Bay.

Charles Sabukewicz is a retired English teacher and spends summers with his wife at their very rural "camp" on Coles Pond in the Northeast Kingdom of Vermont. He's presently rebuilding an old dock and revising some of his longer poems. He was pleased that John Ashbery recently selected one of his poems as one of ten honorable mentions in the 2001 Robert Penn Warren Awards, sponsored by New England Writers. He has a poem entitled "Dreamer/Watcher" coming out in the *Northern New England Review.* Other publications that have published his work include *Poem, Small Pond,* and *Lyric.*

Jan Zlotnik Schmidt is professor of English and coordinator of the Composition Program at the State University of New York at New Paltz. She has published extensively in the field of writing theory and instruction and has given presentations and workshops at the local, regional, and national levels. A published poet, her work has appeared in many journals including *Kansas Quarterly, Cream City Review, Alaska Quarterly Review, Wind,* and *Chiron Review.* Her publications include two volumes of poetry, *We Speak in Tongues* and *She Had This Memory* (Edwin Mellen Press); a multicultural literature anthology, *Legacies,* coauthored with the late Dr. Carley Bogarad (Harcourt Brace); *Women/Writing/Teaching* (SUNY Press); and *Wise Women: Reflections of Teachers at Midlife,* coauthored with Dr. Phyllis R. Freeman (Routledge).

Yvette A. Schnoeker-Shorb is copublisher of Native West Press. In addition, she is engaged in research within the interdisciplinary perspective of ecosemantics, as well as serving as a mentor for both linguistics and poetry courses in the Adult Degree Program at Prescott College. Over the last two decades, her poetry has appeared in *Weber Studies: Voices and Viewpoints of the Contemporary West, Green Hills Literary Lantern, Slant: A Journal of Poetry, So to Speak: A Feminist Journal of Language and Art, Midwest Quarterly, Mid-American Poetry Review, Eureka Literary Magazine, Clackamas Literary Review,* and many other literary journals. In order to balance the many cultural abstractions that dictate each day, she often finds herself affiliating quietly within the biosemantic realm of nature.

Robert Schuler has had ten collections of his poems published. He is at work on a written "Book of Hours" that will contain about one thousand poems and a poetic novel about artists and writers. His work appears in two major anthologies of Midwestern literature, *Inheriting the Earth* and *Imagining Home,* both published by the University of Minnesota Press.

John T. Selawsky was born in Brooklyn, New York, in 1952. He has been writing seriously for almost twenty-five years, with well over one hundred poems published in a variety of journals, publications, and anthologies. He has lived in Berkeley, California, since 1987 with his wife and son. He is an editor by profession and was elected to the Berkeley school board in November 2000 for a four-year term.

Roger Sheffer teaches writing at Minnesota State University at Mankato. His most recent publications are articles in *Adirondack Life* and *Appalachia.* His third fiction collection, *Music of the Inner Lakes,* was published in 1999 by New Rivers Press.

Neil Shepard has published two books of poetry, *Scavenging the Country for a Heartbeat* (winner of the First Book Award, Mid-List Press, 1993) and *I'm Here Because I Lost My Way* (Mid-List Press, 1998). His poems are forthcoming or have recently appeared in the *Paris Review, Ploughshares, Boulevard, Triquarterly,* and *Ontario Review.* He teaches in the B.F.A. writing program at Johnson State College in Vermont and edits the *Green Mountain Review.*

Vivian Shipley, editor of *Connecticut Review,* is a Connecticut State University Distinguished Professor. In 2001, she won the Robert Frost Foundation Poetry Award, the Daniel Varoujan Award from the New England Poetry Club, and the *Charter Oak Review* Poetry Prize from the University of Connecticut. In 2000, she won the Marble Faun Award for Poetry from the William Faulkner Society, the *Thin Air Magazine* Poetry Prize from Northern Arizona University, and was named faculty scholar at Southern Connecticut State University where she teaches creative writing. She has also won the Lucille Medwick Award from the Poetry Society of America, the Ann Stanford Prize from the University of Southern California, the Reader's Choice Award from *Prairie Schooner,* the *Sonora Review* Poetry Prize from the University of Arizona, the *So To Speak* Poetry Prize from George Mason University, the Elinor Benedict Poetry Prize from *Passages North,* the John Z. Bennett Award for Poetry from University of Southern Louisiana, and the Hackney Literary Award for Poetry from Birmingham-Southern College. She has published nine books of poetry. Her tenth book, *When There Is No Shore,* won the 2002 Word Press Poetry Prize.

Mason Smith's novel *Everybody Knows and Nobody Cares* was published by Knopf in 1971. He is writes for a number of magazines and earns his living as a boat builder.

Noel Smith worked as a social worker for eastern Kentucky's Frontier Nursing Service in the 1950s and 1960s, reaching her clients by jeep and by horseback. After that, she raised a daughter and taught elementary school in Suffern, New York. She lives with her husband in the lower Hudson Valley and spends as much time outdoors as possible. She is currently working on a series of poems and oral histories of people from the Appalachian region. She has published in numerous literary journals, including *West Branch, Yankee Magazine, Riverwind,* and *Creative Woman.*

Matthew J. Spireng's poetry has appeared in many journals, including *American Scholar, Amicus Journal, Southern Humanities Review, Tampa Review, Yankee, Poet Lore, Southern Poetry Review, High Plains Literary Review,* and *College English.* "Out of Body," a collection of his poems, was a finalist for the 1998 Cleveland State University Poetry Center Prize and two other national contests.

Susan Fantl Spivack is a writer and storyteller who tells traditional and contemporary tales; oral histories of the Holocaust and World War II, the Vietnam War, and the Civil Rights Movement; and her own stories and poems to audiences of all ages. She teaches the craft of poetry writing to children and adults. Her poems and stories have appeared in numerous literary magazines and anthologies. Her Singing Frog Press has published handmade chapbooks including *Times River: A Calendar of Poems* (twelve chapbooks, a month of poems per book) and eight other handsewn collections of poetry.

Alan Steinberg, who earned his doctorate from Carnegie Mellon University, is an associate professor in the Department of English and Communication at SUNY Potsdam. His books include *Divided,* a collection of short stories, and *Cry of the Leopard,* a novel. In addition to recently published fiction in *Peregrine,* his poetry collection *Fathering* won the Seventh Annual National Poetry Chapbook competition sponsored by the Sarasota Poetry Theatre Press.

Barry Sternlieb's work has appeared in *Poetry, Gettysburg Review, Prairie Schooner, Quarterly West, Yankee, Wilderness, Country Journal,* and others. His latest book is *Thoreau's Hat* (Brooding Heron Press, 1994). He also edits Mad River Press, specializing in letterpress poetry prints and chapbooks since 1986.

Tim Strong graduated from the State University of New York at Plattsburgh with highest honors. He went on to receive his master's degree in English and creative writing from Binghamton University. Strong's poems and stories have been published in literary journals such as the *Alabama Review* and the *Mississippi Review.* His work has been included in several anthologies of poetry as well. He is seeking a publisher for his novel, "The Whippoorwill Chronicles." An entrepreneur, Strong owns and manages his own business, the Birchbark Bookshop, currently offering fifty thousand used and rare books.

Anthony O. Tyler is a professor in the Department of English and Communication at SUNY Potsdam, specializing in British Romantic literature, film and fiction, nature literature, and the nineteenth-century British novel. He is the recipient of the college's Excellence in Teaching Award. He was the editor of *Blueline* from 1989 to 1998 and continues to serve on its editorial board.

Desire Vail lives in the hills south of Bath, New York. Her chapbook *See How Wet the Street Sounds* was published by Foothills Publications.

Sarah Van Arsdale's first novel, *Toward Amnesia,* was published by Riverhead/Putnam. She lives in northern Vermont and New York City, where she writes and teaches creative writing.

Gale Warner was a poet and freelance environmental journalist who also published two books about Soviet-American citizen diplomacy before her death at the age of thirty. *Dancing at the Edge of Life,* her memoir of her final illness, was published in 1998. She won an Academy of American Poets contest in 1985, and her poems have appeared in a number of magazines including *Agni* and *West Branch.*

Malcolm Willison was born long ago in the shadow of Sing-Sing, at a time when his mother could still see the prisoners breaking rocks with sledgehammers. He edited his college literary magazine, *The Dodo* (long since extinct), but refused to write poetry until it forced him to in his twenties. Some has been published here and there and read at formal readings now and again. A long-time member of the Washout Poetry group, he has taken part in a workshop of John Montague's, and studied haiku with Stephen Gill in Kyoto in 2000. He at last admits, as a sometime resident for thirty-five years, that he is indeed a citizen of Schenectady, New York, from where he can go hiking and climbing to expand on childhood summer camp vistas in the Adirondacks' High Peaks. He also teaches comparative and historical sociology, and occasionally peace studies, in the United States and Brazil, and is a manuscript editor in the social sciences and related and applied fields.

Elizabeth Woodbury is a musician, composer, poet, and educator living in Saratoga Springs, New York.

Marly Youmans is a South Carolina native currently living in Cooperstown, New York, with her husband and three children. She has published poetry in many magazines and anthologies. Her novels are: *The Wolf Pit* (Farrar, Strauss, and Giroux, 2001); *Catherwood* (Farrar, Straus, and Giroux, 1996); and *Little Jordan* (David R. Godine, 1995). A novel for children, *The Curse of the Raven Mocker*, is forthcoming from Farrar, Straus, and Giroux Books for Young Readers.

Frederick Zydek is the author of four collections of poetry: *Lights Along the Missouri, Storm Warning, Ending the Fast,* and *The Conception Abbey Poems.* His work appears in the *Antioch Review, Hollins Critic, Michigan Quarterly Review, Poetry, Poetry Northwest,* and other journals. Formerly a professor of creative writing and theology at the University of Nebraska and later at the College of Saint Mary, he is now a gentleman farmer when he isn't writing. Most recently, he has accepted the post as editor for Lone Willow Press.